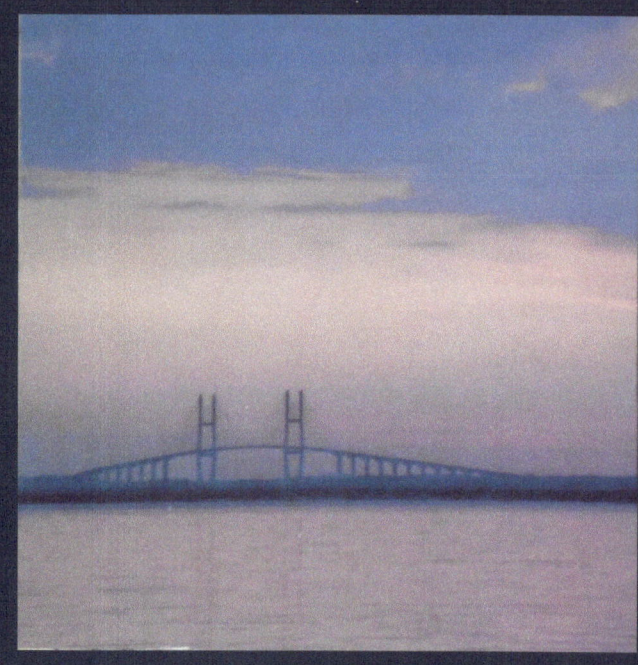

**Sidney Lanier Bridge with Pink Sunset | 2017**
Photo Collage on panel | 6" x 6" | $65.00

# BRIDGES  |

Where will your dreams take you? You can't know the future, but you will cross bridges in your life. A bridge will take you from where you are now to where you want to go. In these pieces, the bridge is a metaphor for the link between your past and your future.

The bridge symbolizes a focused pathway to your dreams. The bridge is the way through and over to the other side; the next part of your life, the beginning of the life you create for yourself.

These bridges are ones I have admired and used in my travels. They vary widely in size and appearance, but they serve a similar purpose in transporting people from one side to other in their travels.

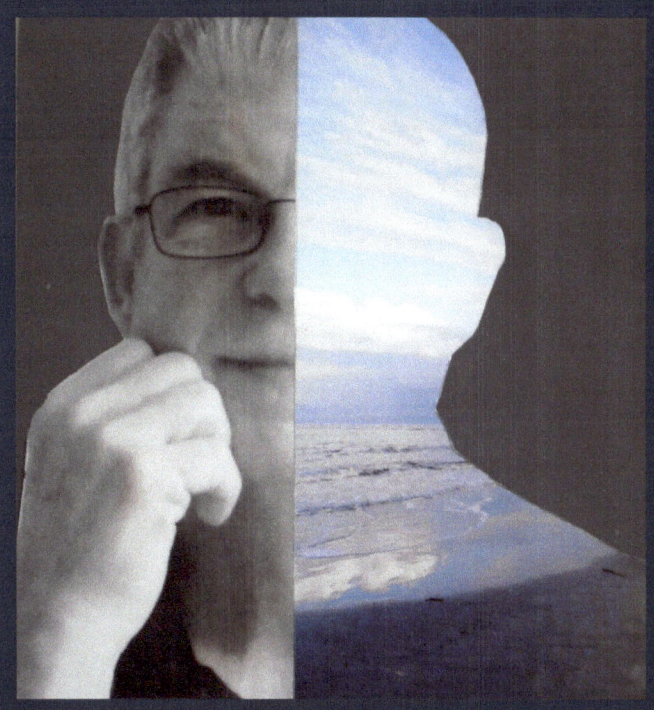

# ABOUT PHOTOCOLLAGES

I look for a scene in which shapes and colors align and converge into an interesting display. If the light and color and space are compelling enough, I want to show the scene over time with multiple photographs.

As I began to put together photo collages of my perceptions of these scenes, I realized that the works expressed the way I see. My mind perceives a whole scene, but my eyes move from part to part focusing on small areas at the time. My mind pulls it together into a coherent image of lines, shapes and colors.

My method of working fits well with digital photography. I zoom in with my camera and take multiple photographs of parts of a scene similar to the way my eyes move through it. I then print out the photos which now are fragments that I arrange into an image that recreates the

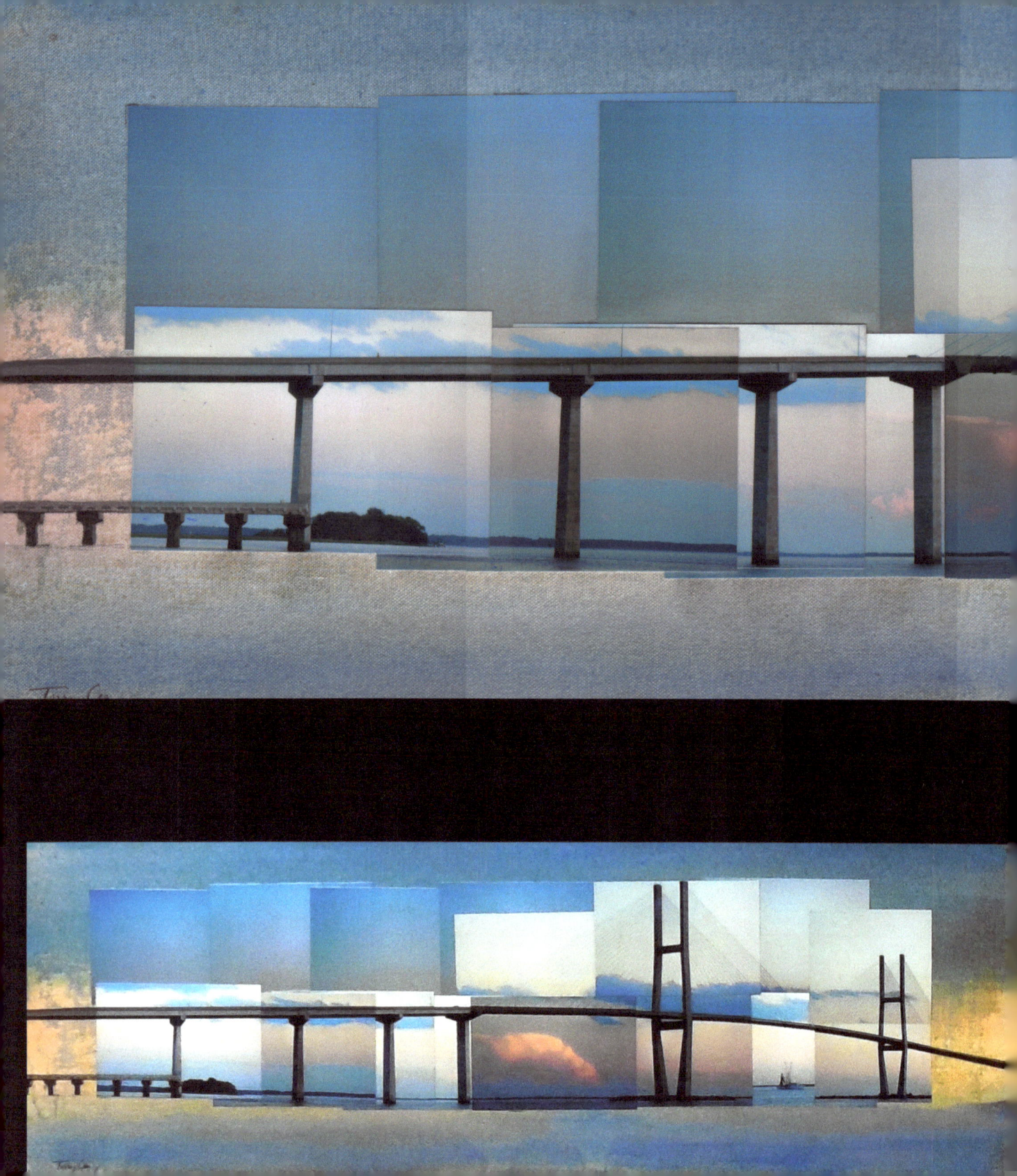

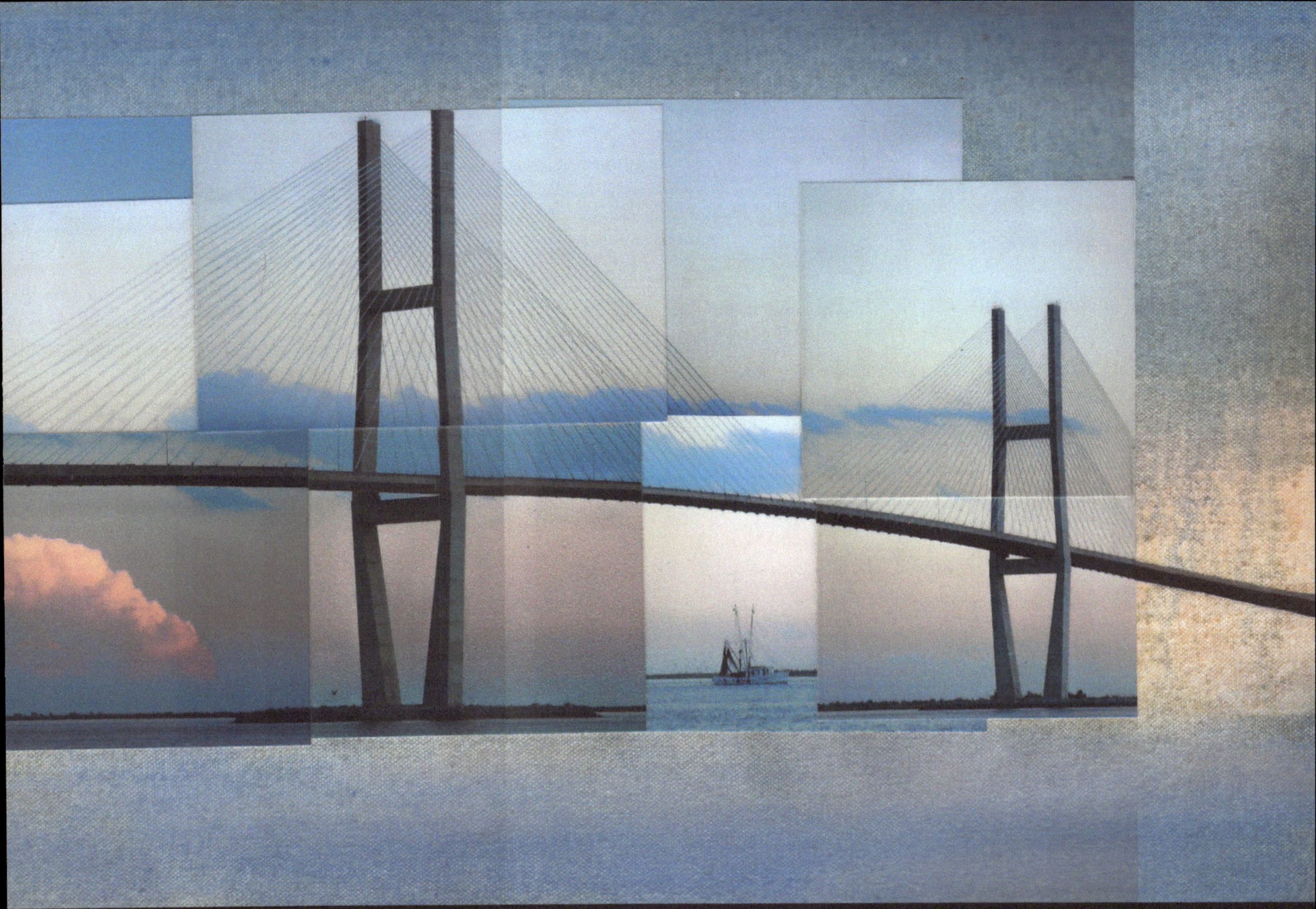

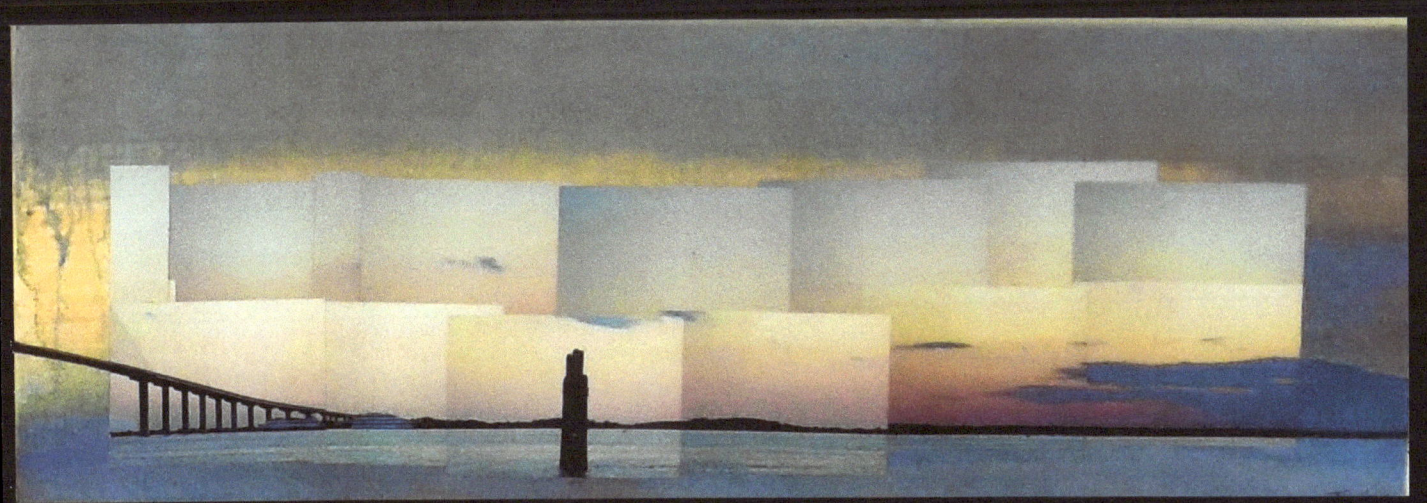

Sidney Lanier Bridge Panorama I

**Sidney Lanier Bridge Panorama I and II** | 2013 | 12" x 72" | Photo collage on canvas | $600.00

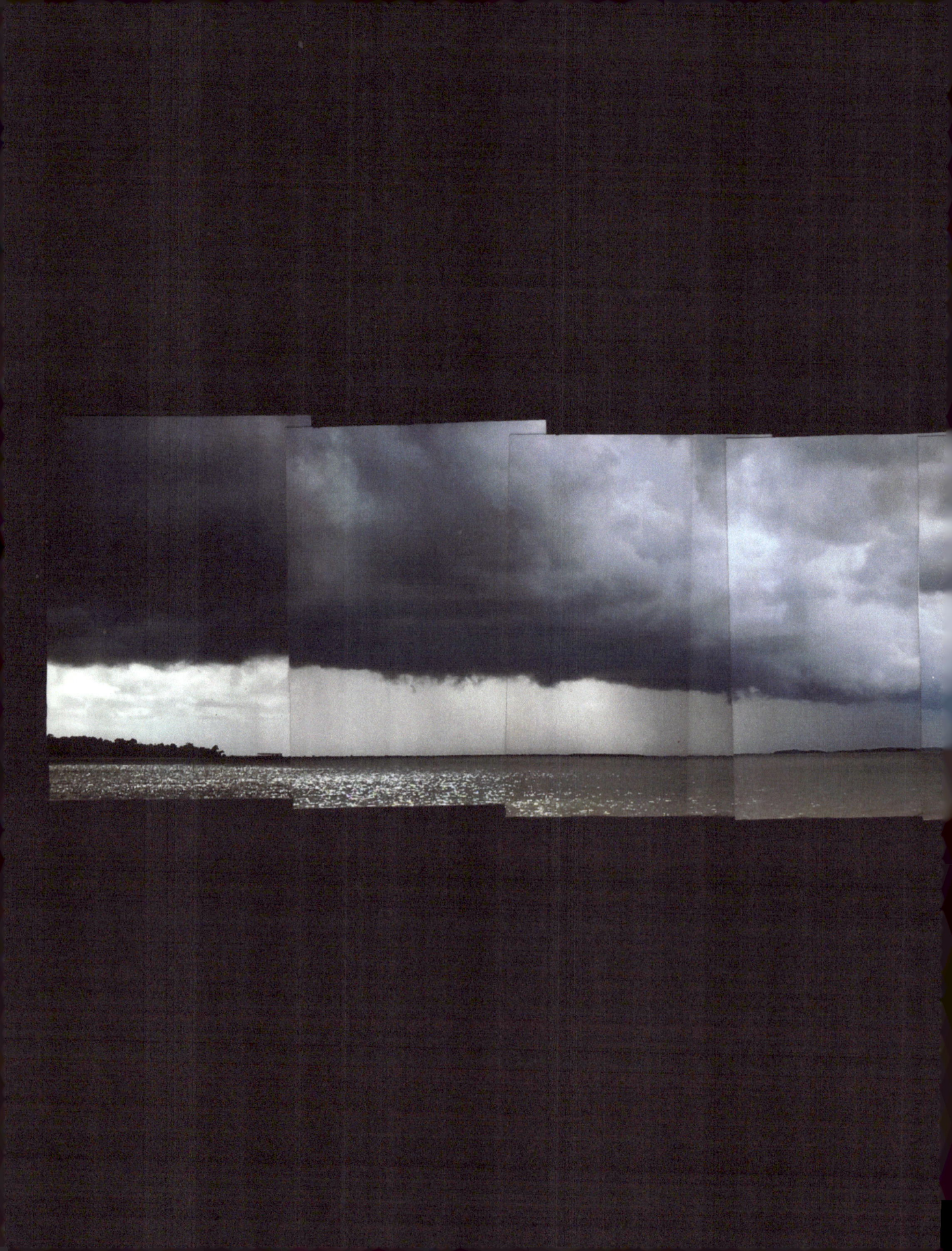

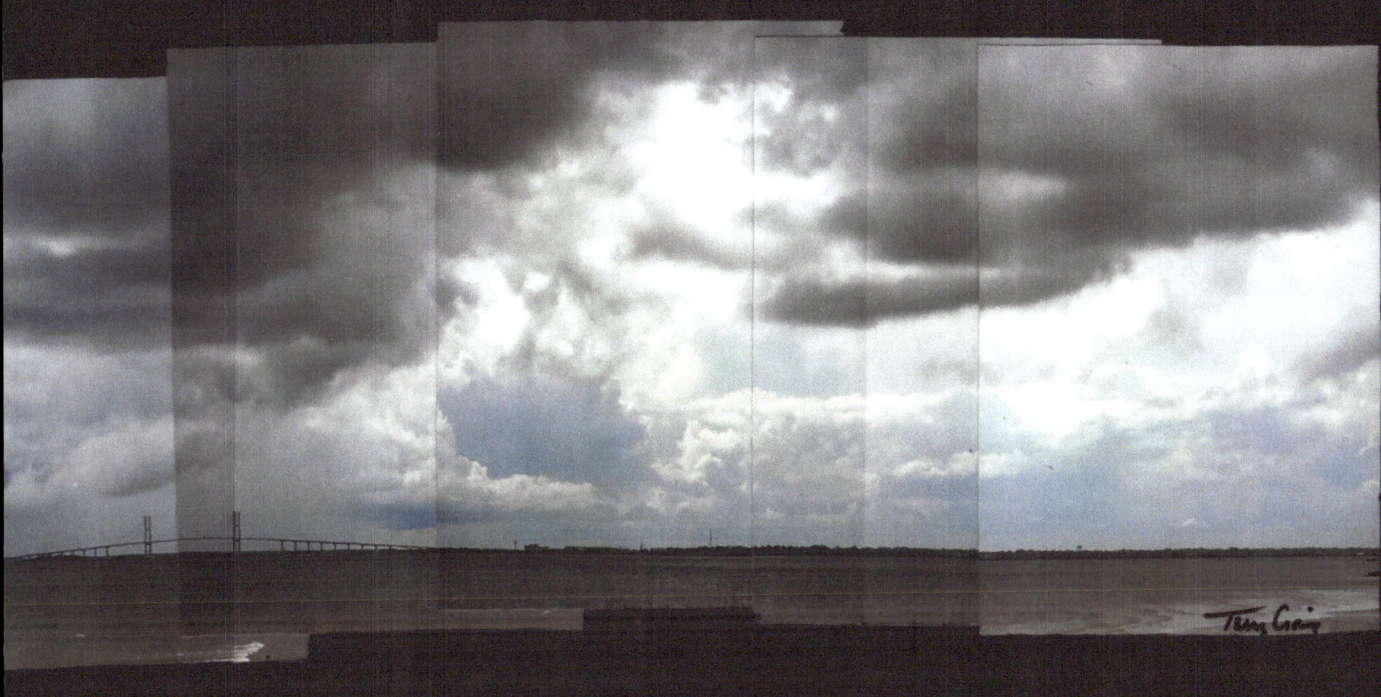

Moving Storm | 2017 | Photocollage on panel | 12" x 40" | $300.00

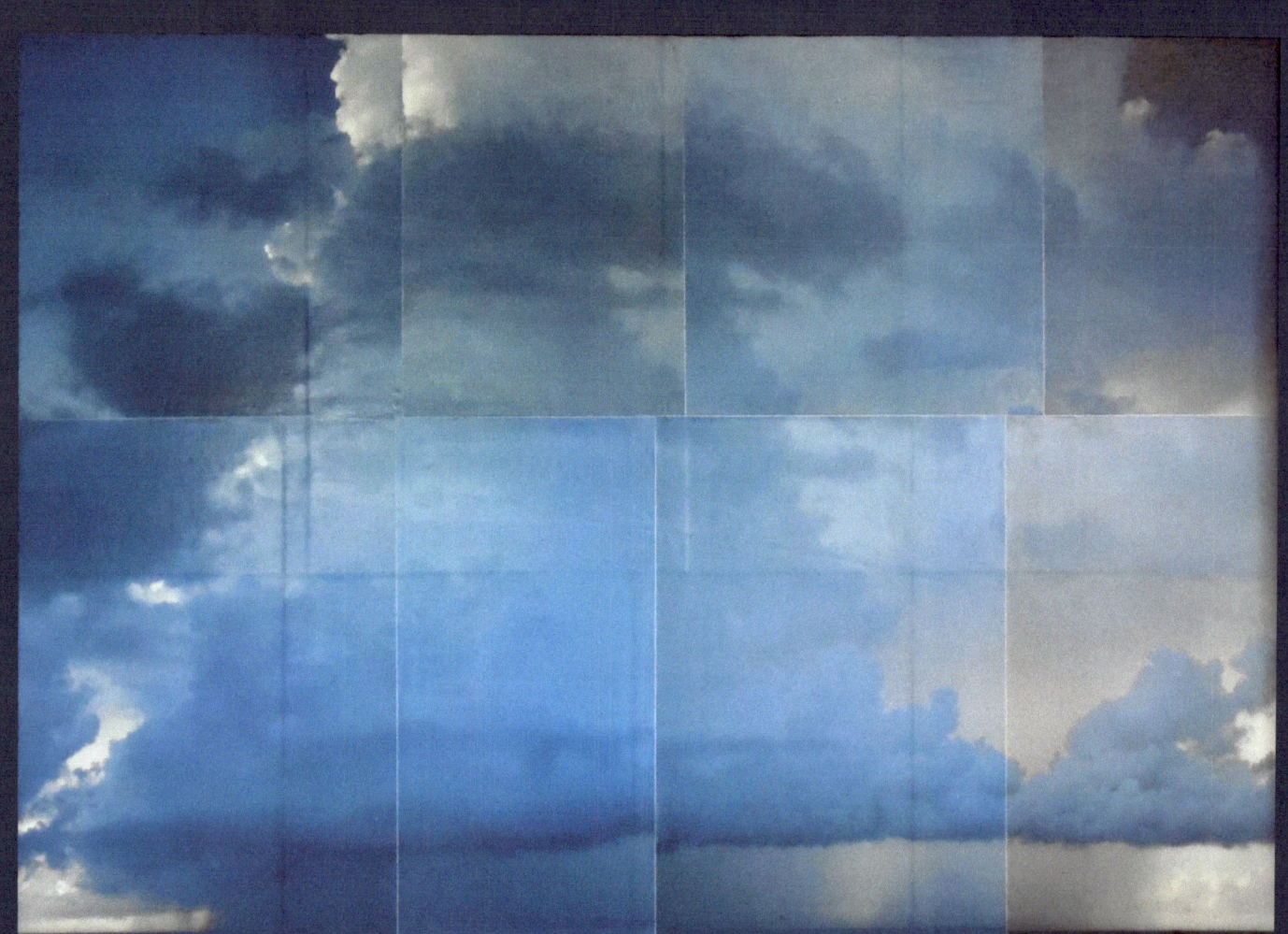

**Blue Squall Hides Bridge**  |  2017  |  Photomontage on panel  |  28" x 40"  |  $350.00

**Sidney Lanier Bridge at Midday**
2014
Mixed media photo collage on canvas
30" x 24"
$400.00

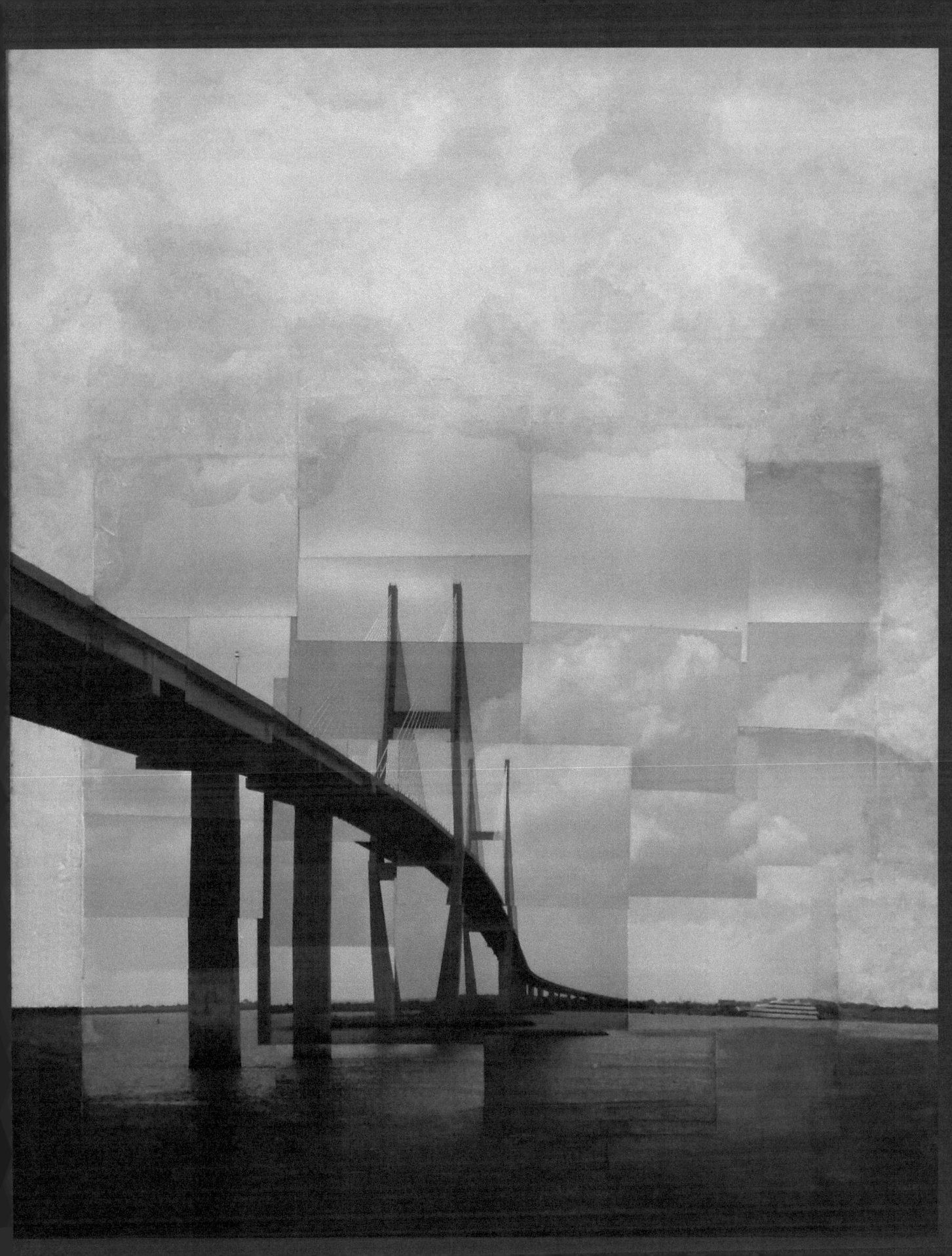

# Thunderstorm Over the Sidney Lanier Bridge

2017 | Photo encaustic on panel | 20" x 16" | $400.00

detail

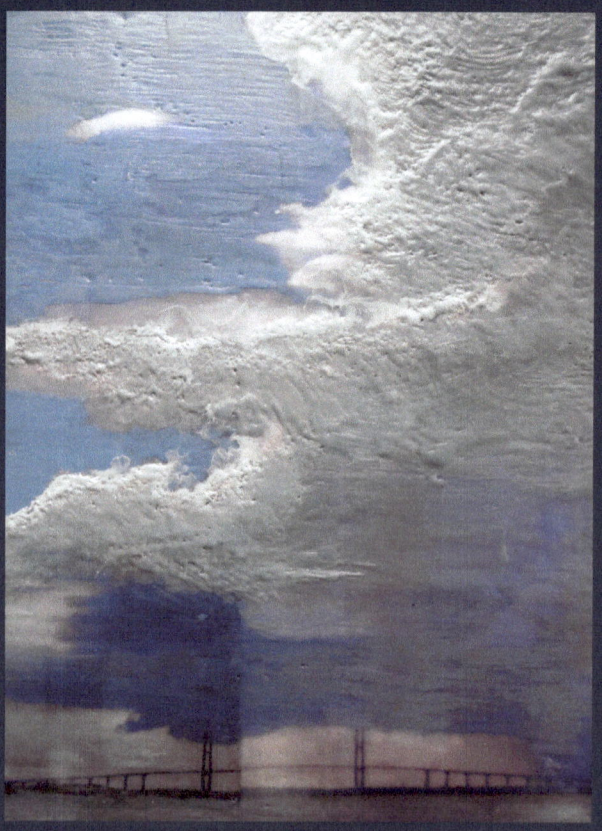

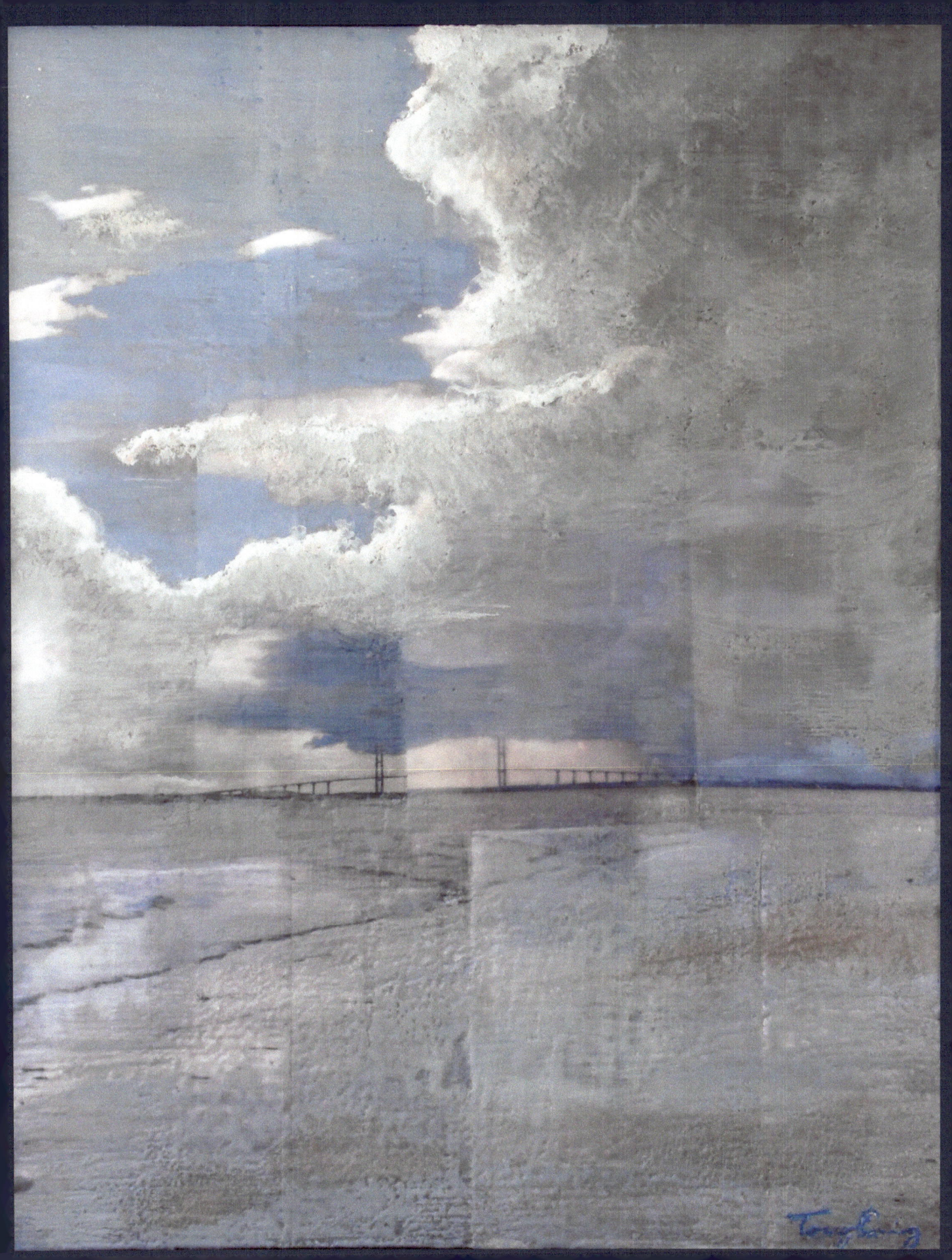

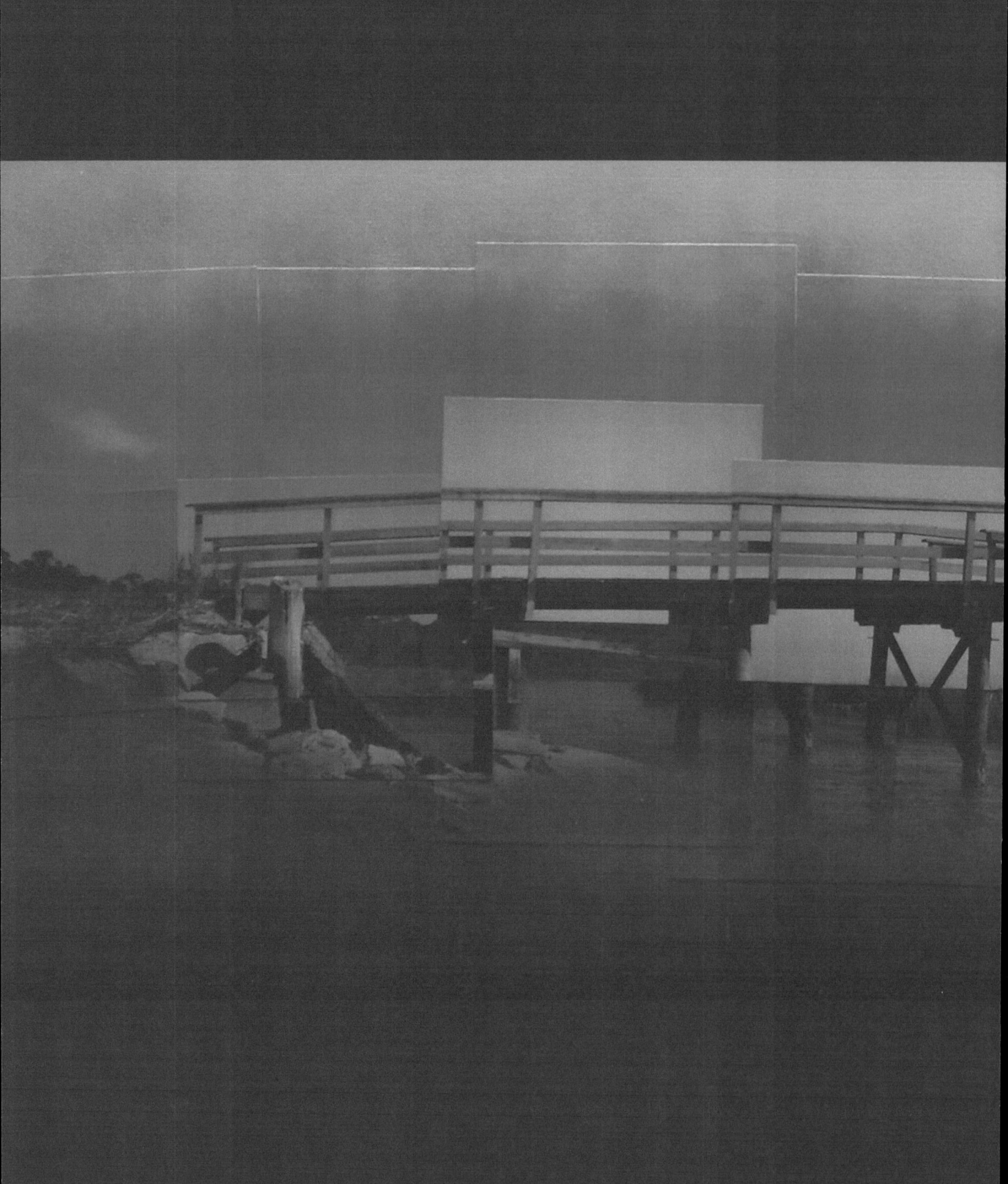

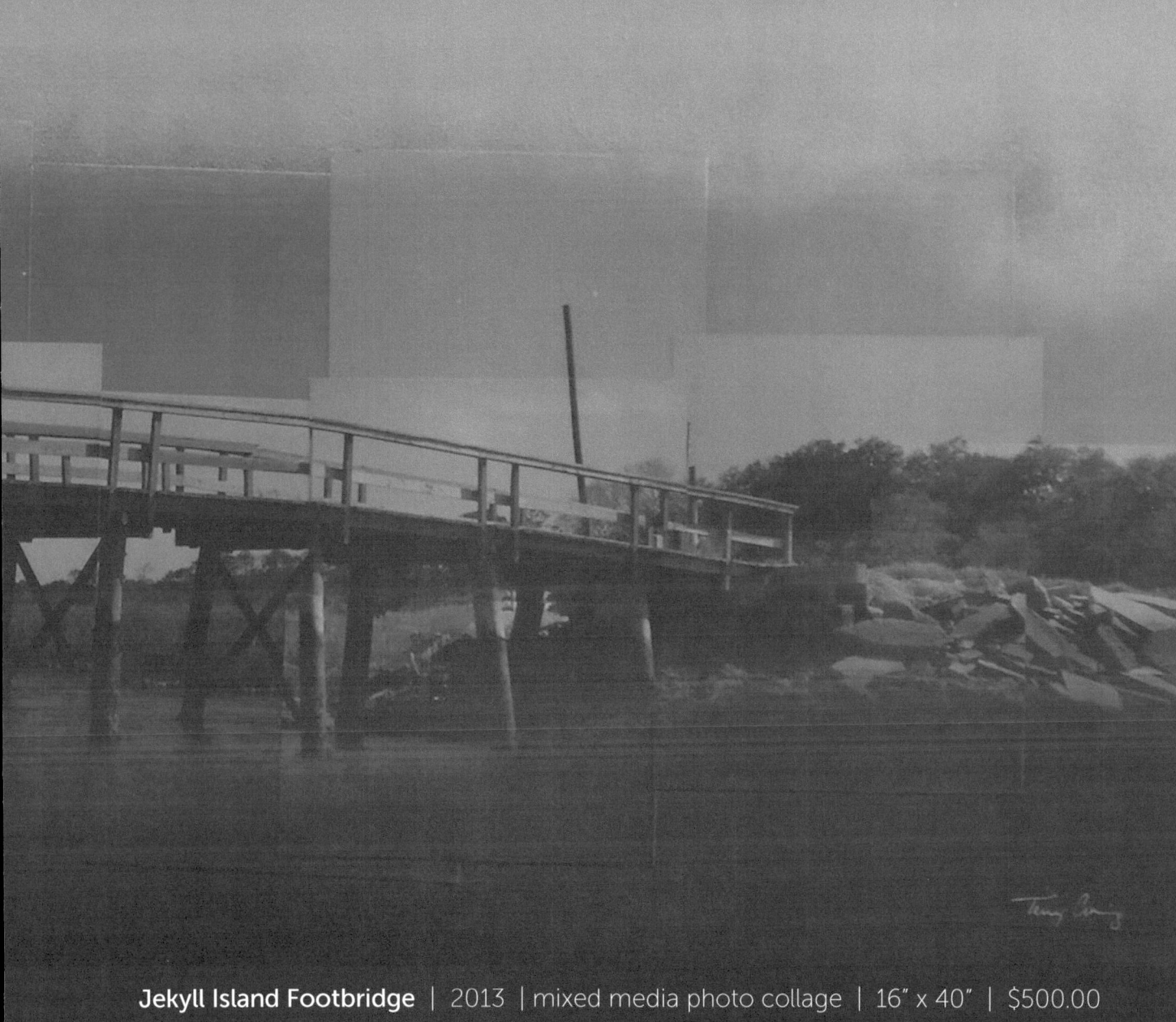

**Jekyll Island Footbridge** | 2013 | mixed media photo collage | 16" x 40" | $500.00

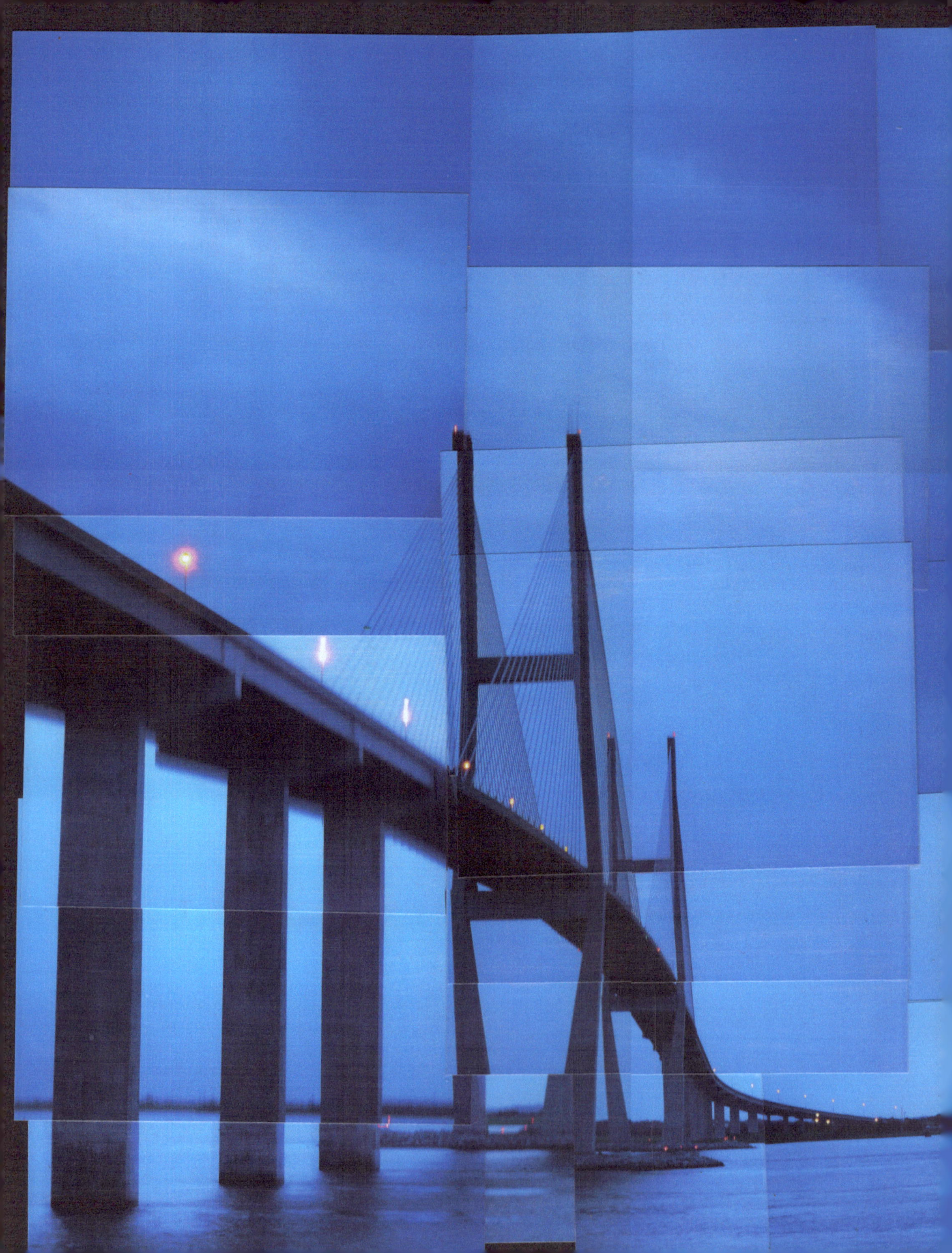

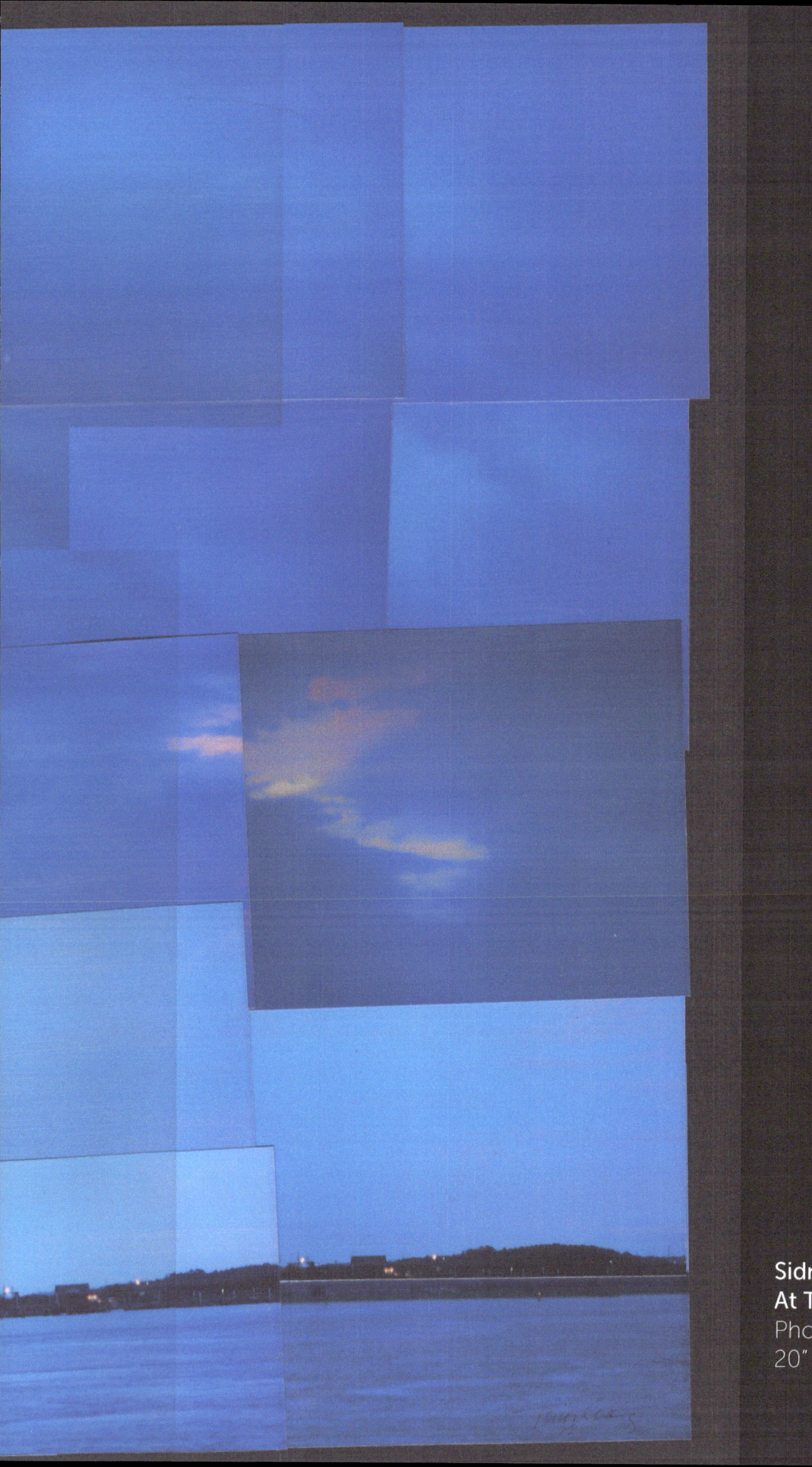

**Sidney Lanier Bridge At Twilight** | 2010
Photocollage on panel
20" x 24" | Sold

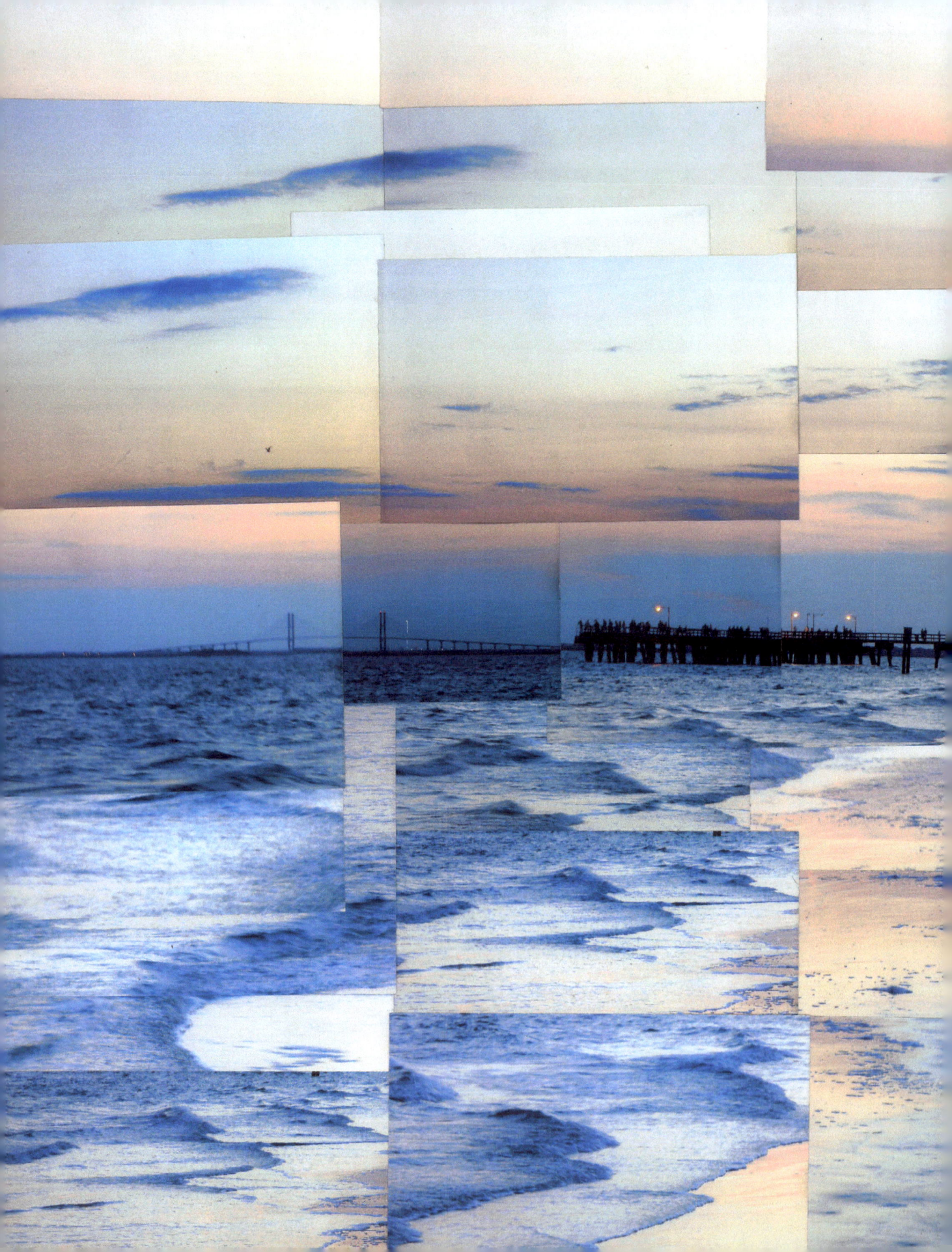

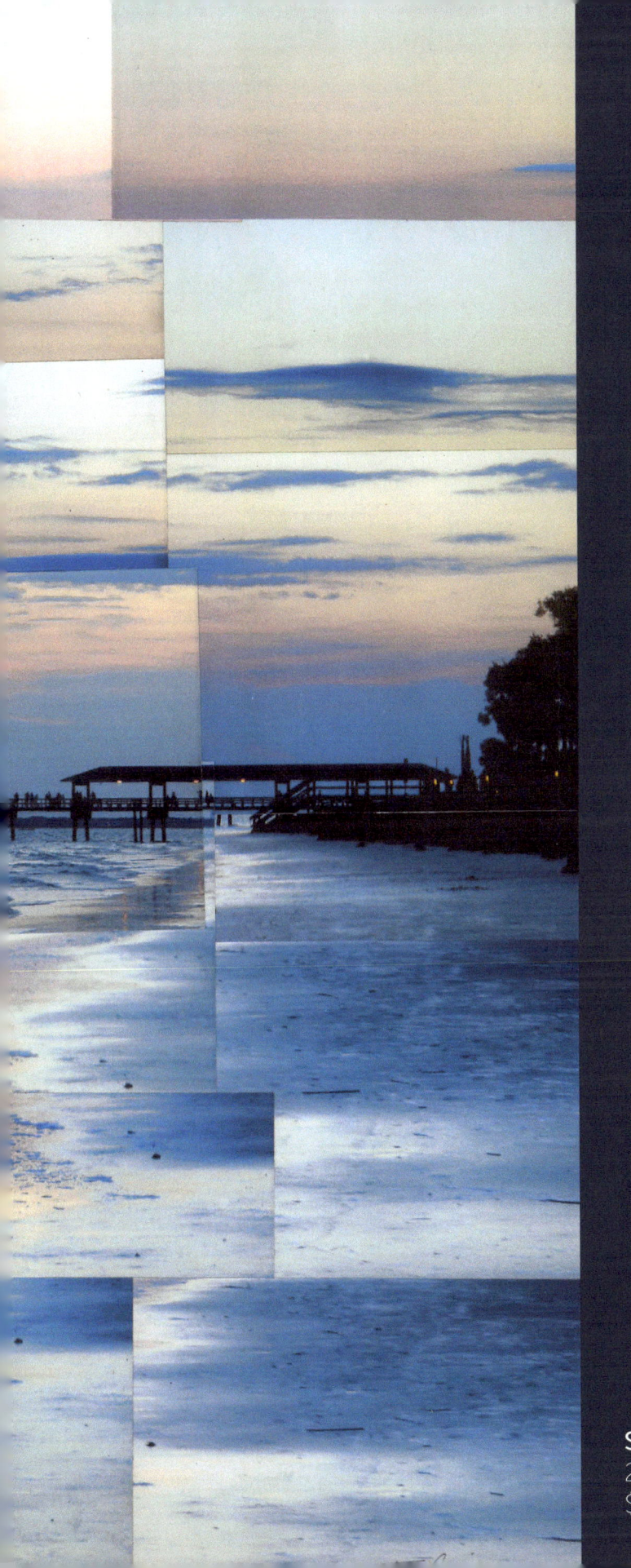

St. Simons Pier at Twilight | 2012
27" x 24" | Photocollage on canvas
$300.00

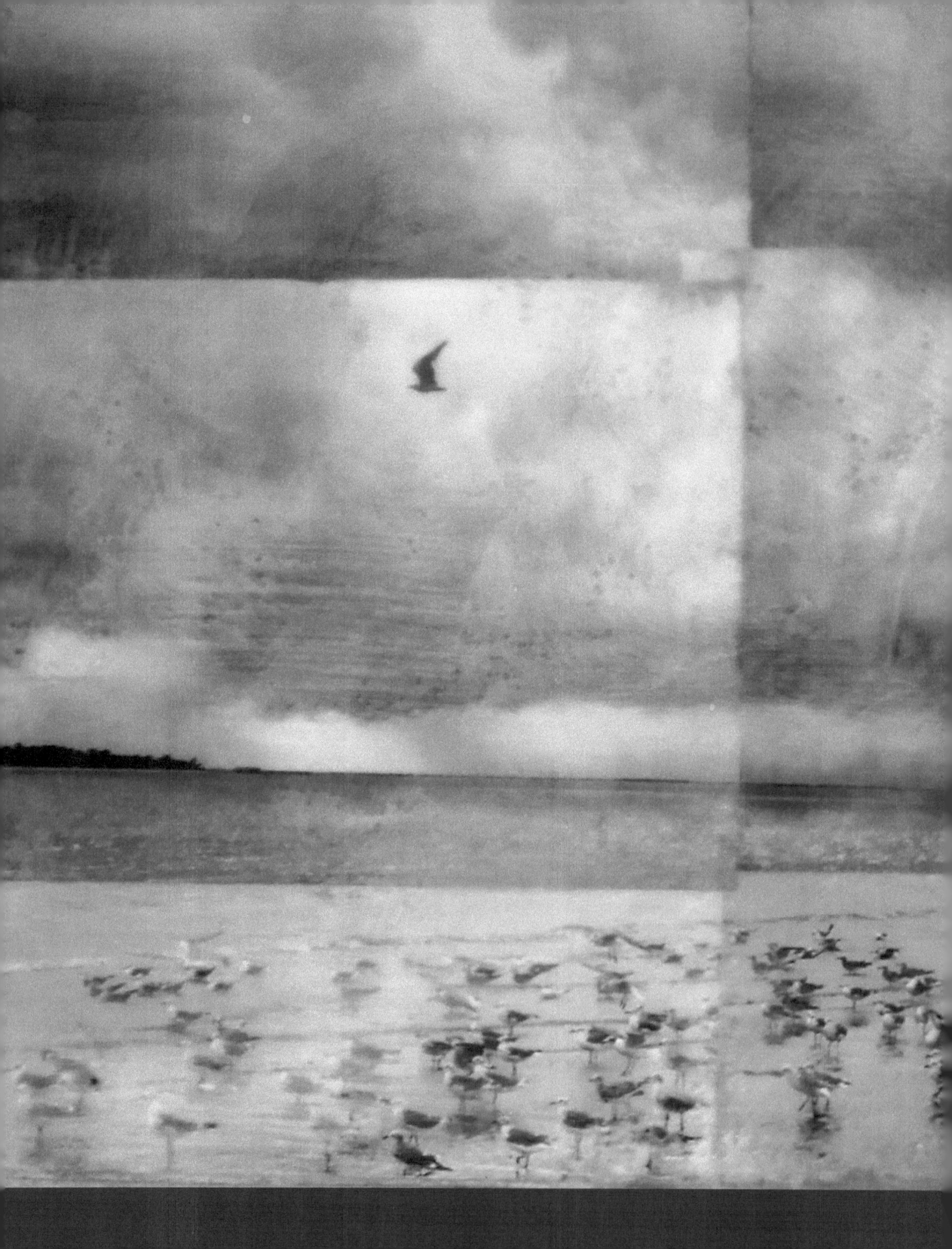

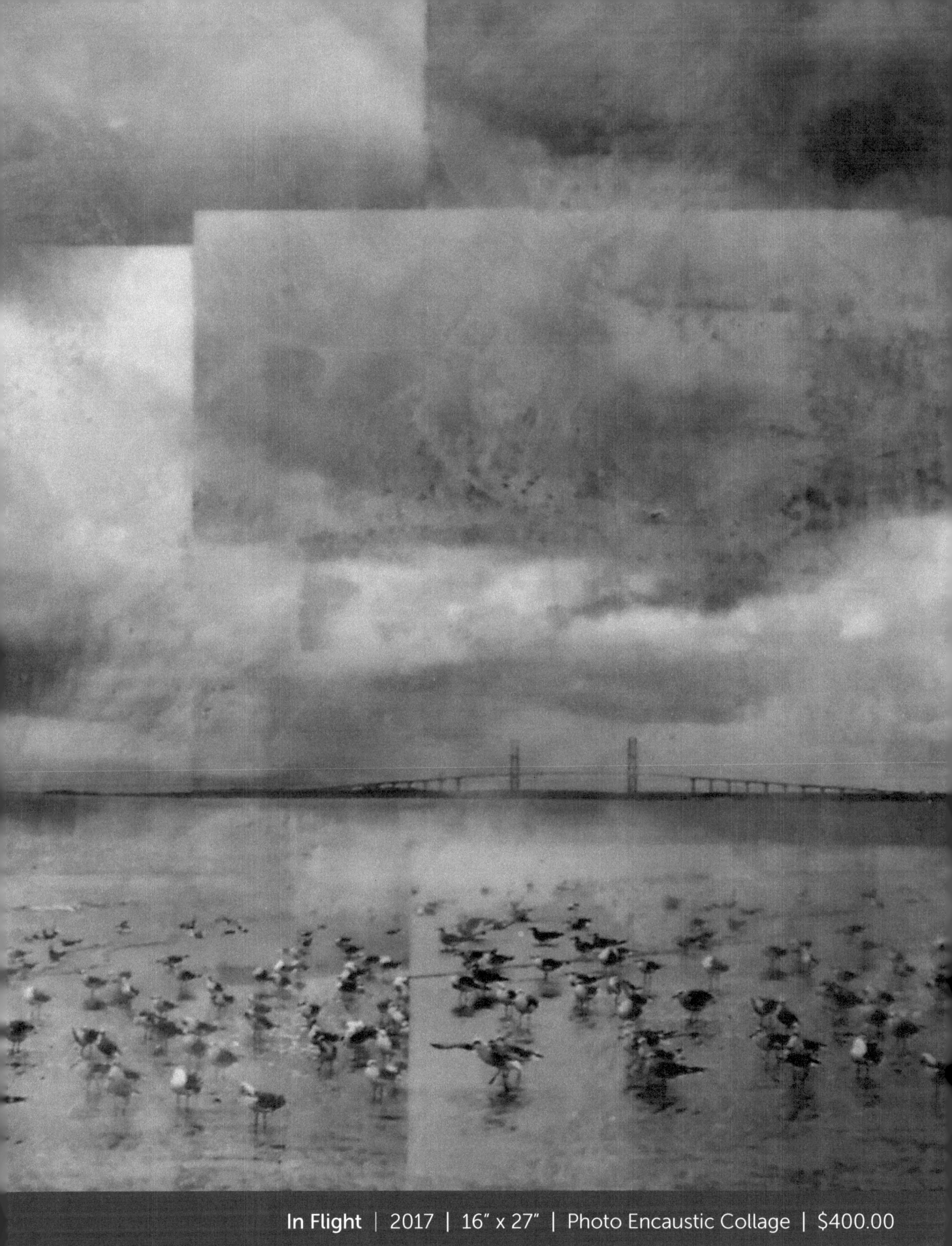
In Flight | 2017 | 16" x 27" | Photo Encaustic Collage | $400.00

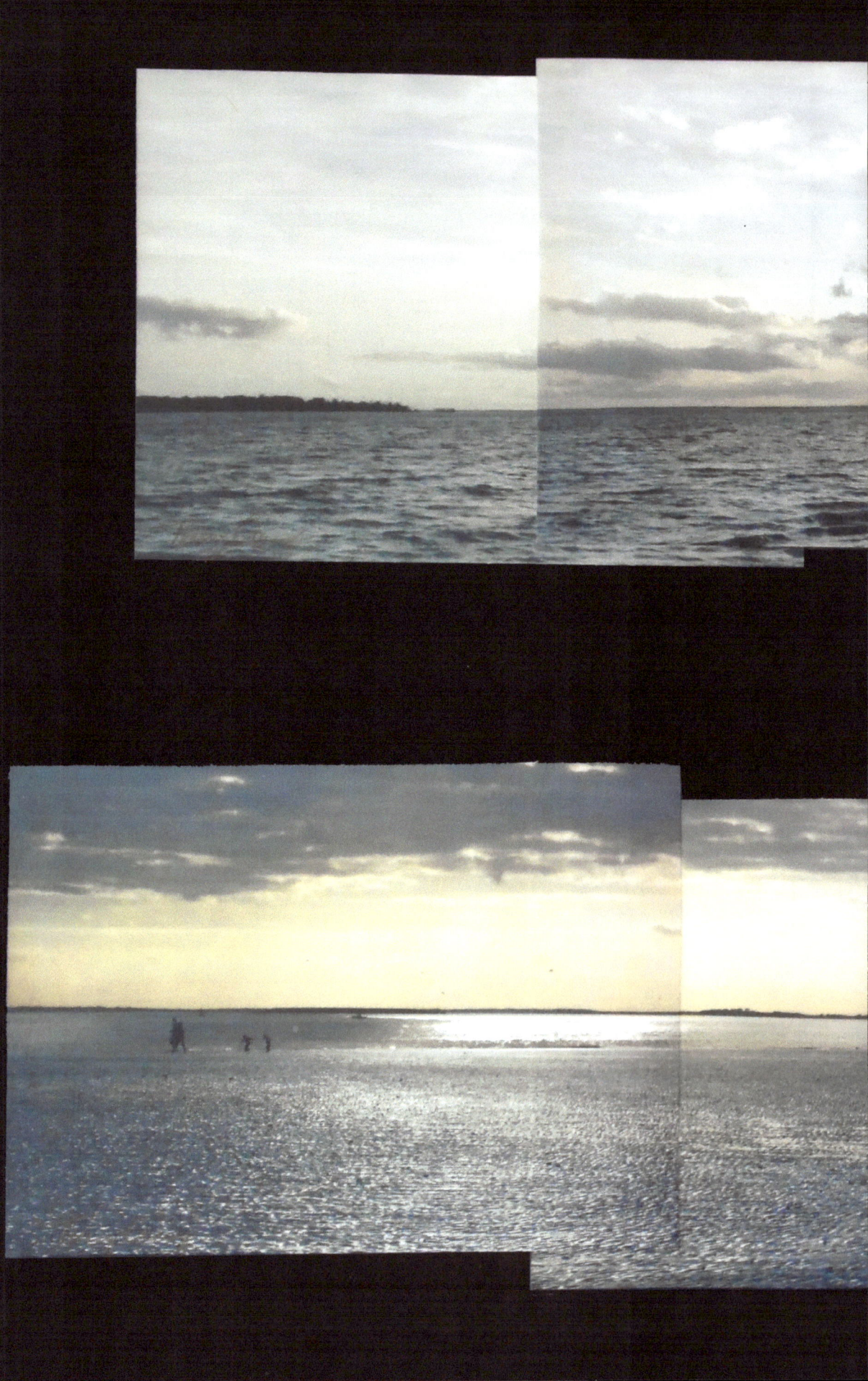

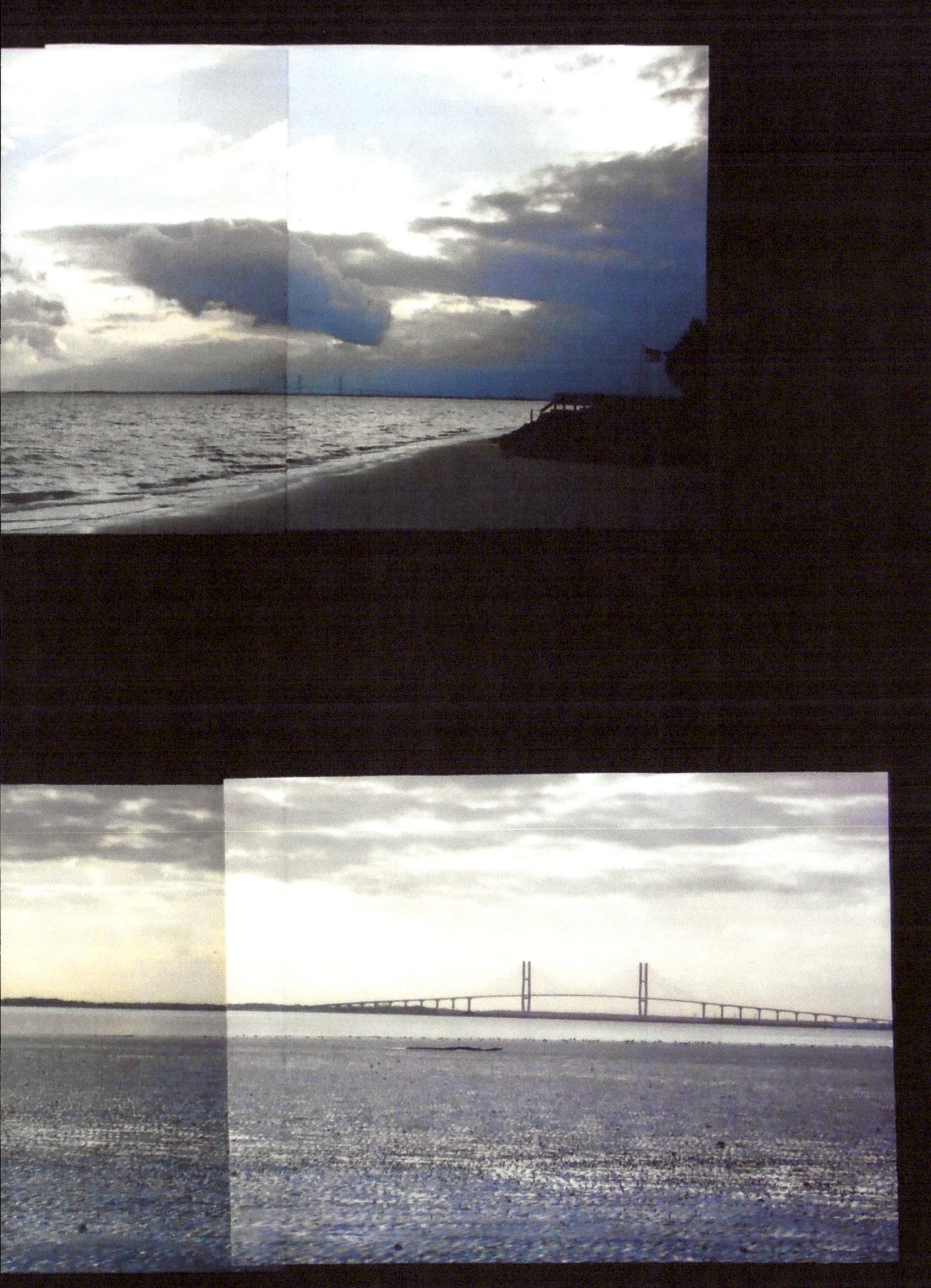

Sidney Lanier Bridge – Double Sunsets | 2017
16" x 20" | Photo collage on panel | $200.00

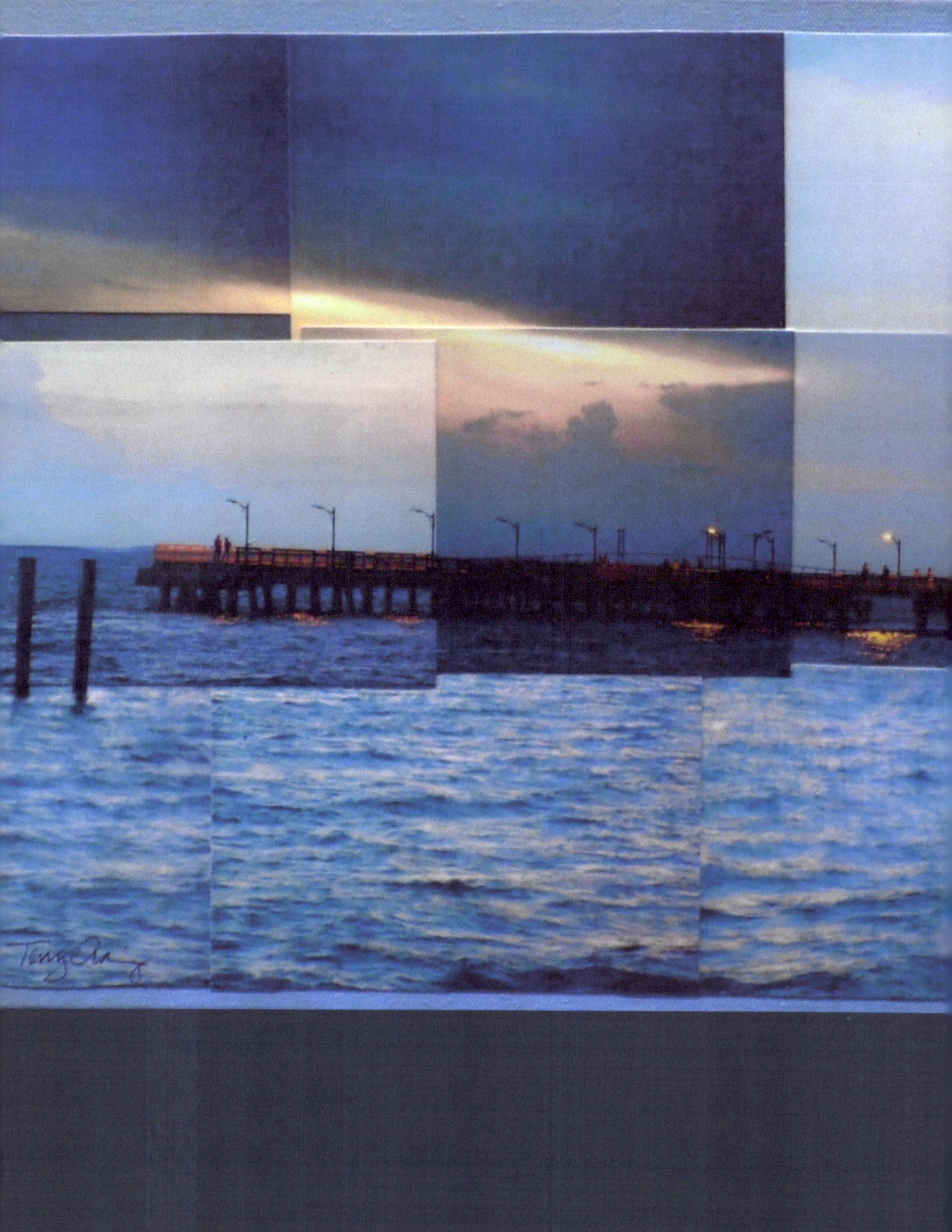

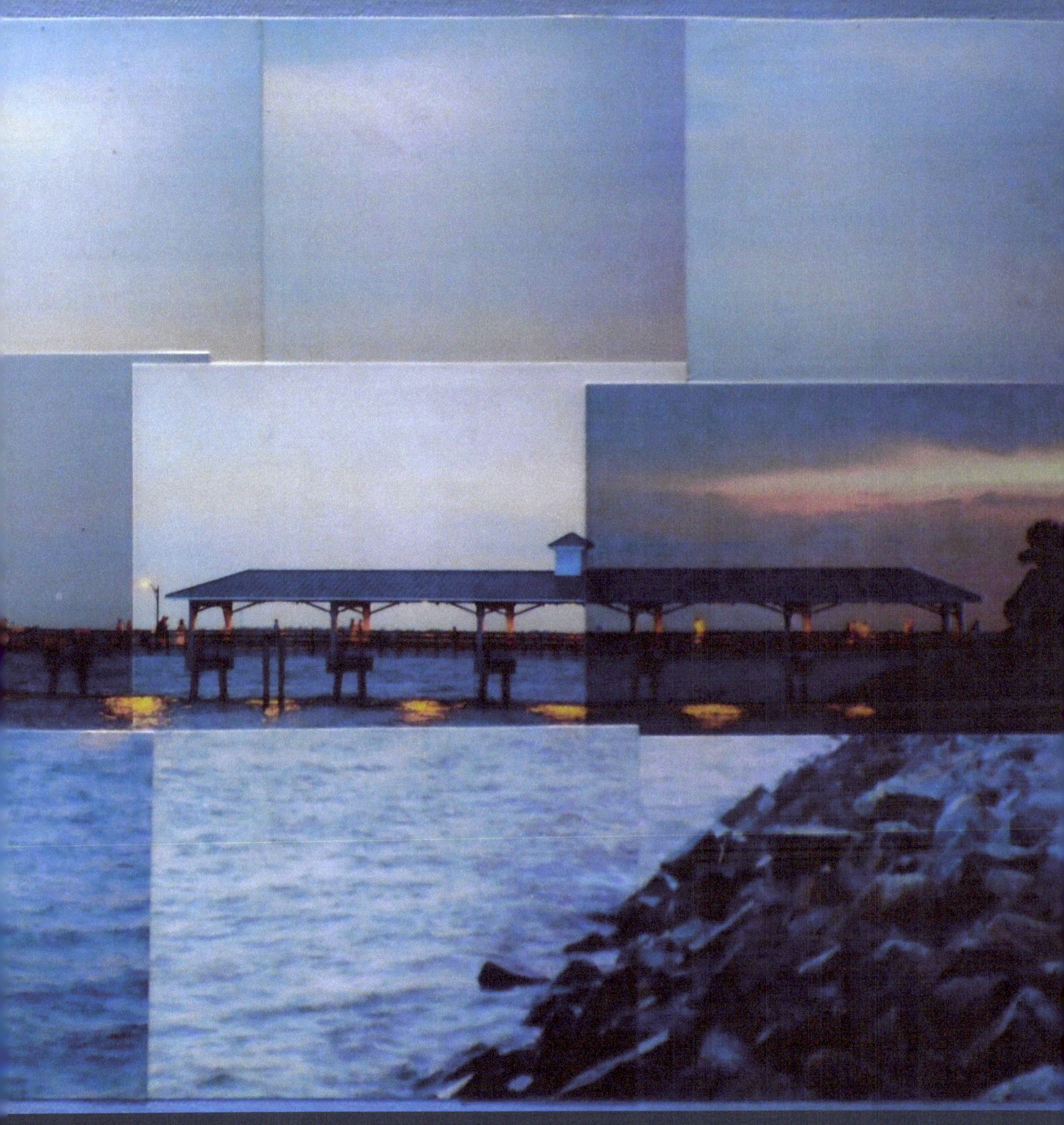
St. Simons Pier at Sunset | 2013 | 12" x 24" | Photo collage on canvas | $200.00

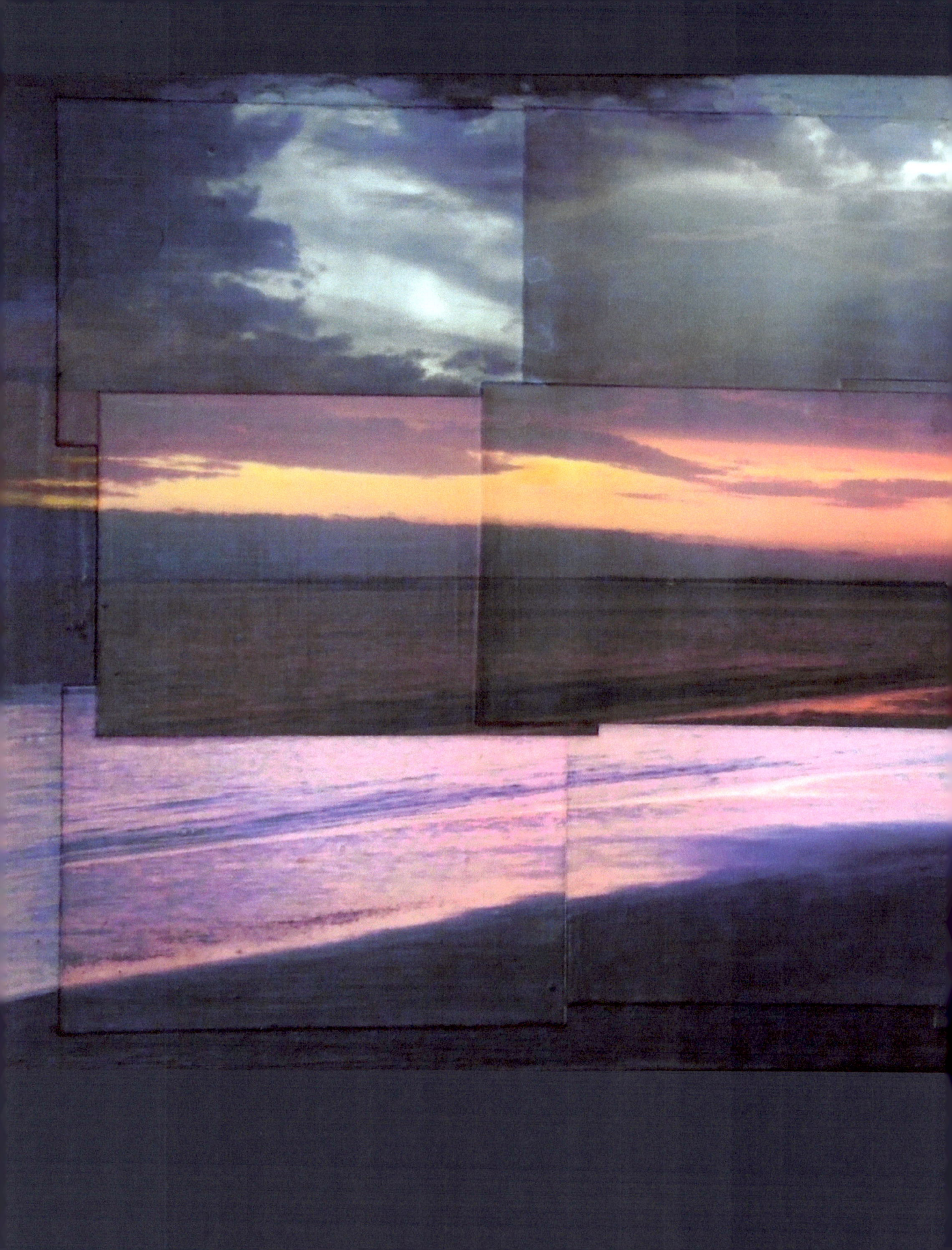

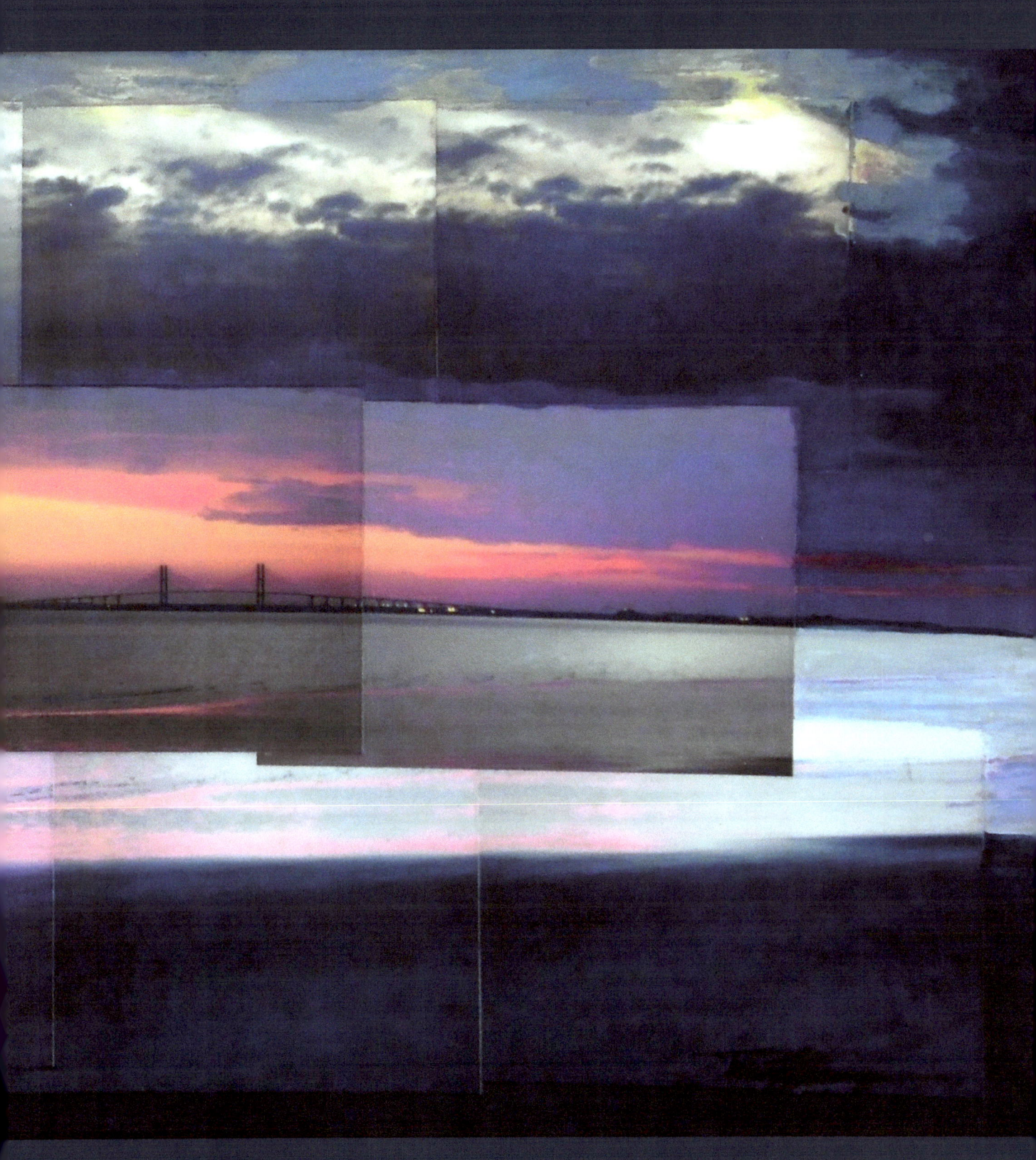

Sunset Reflections | 2012 | 12" x 24" | Mixed-media photo collage on canvas | $200.00

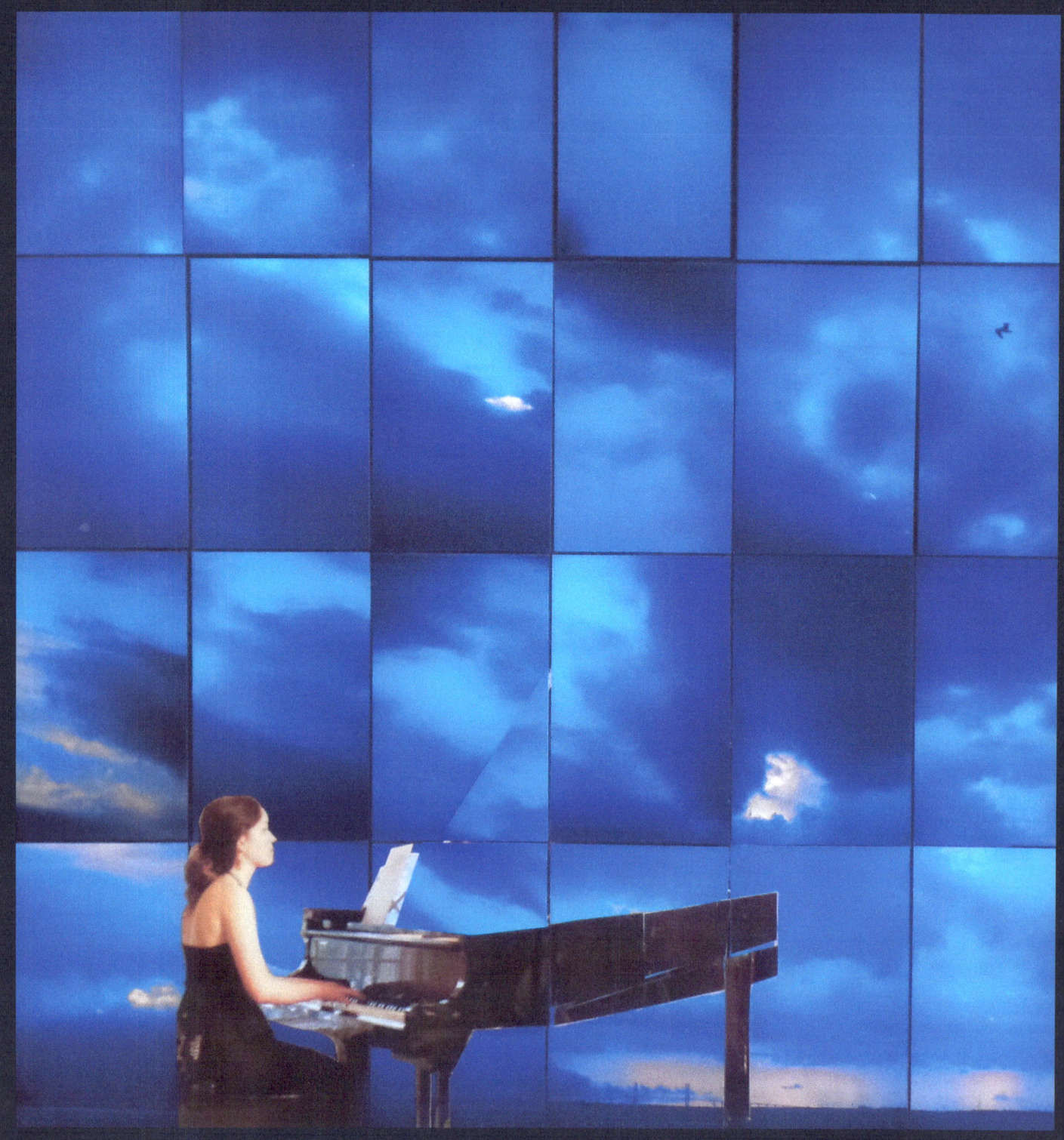

Nocturne | 2015 | 24" x 24" | Photo collage on canvas | $250.00

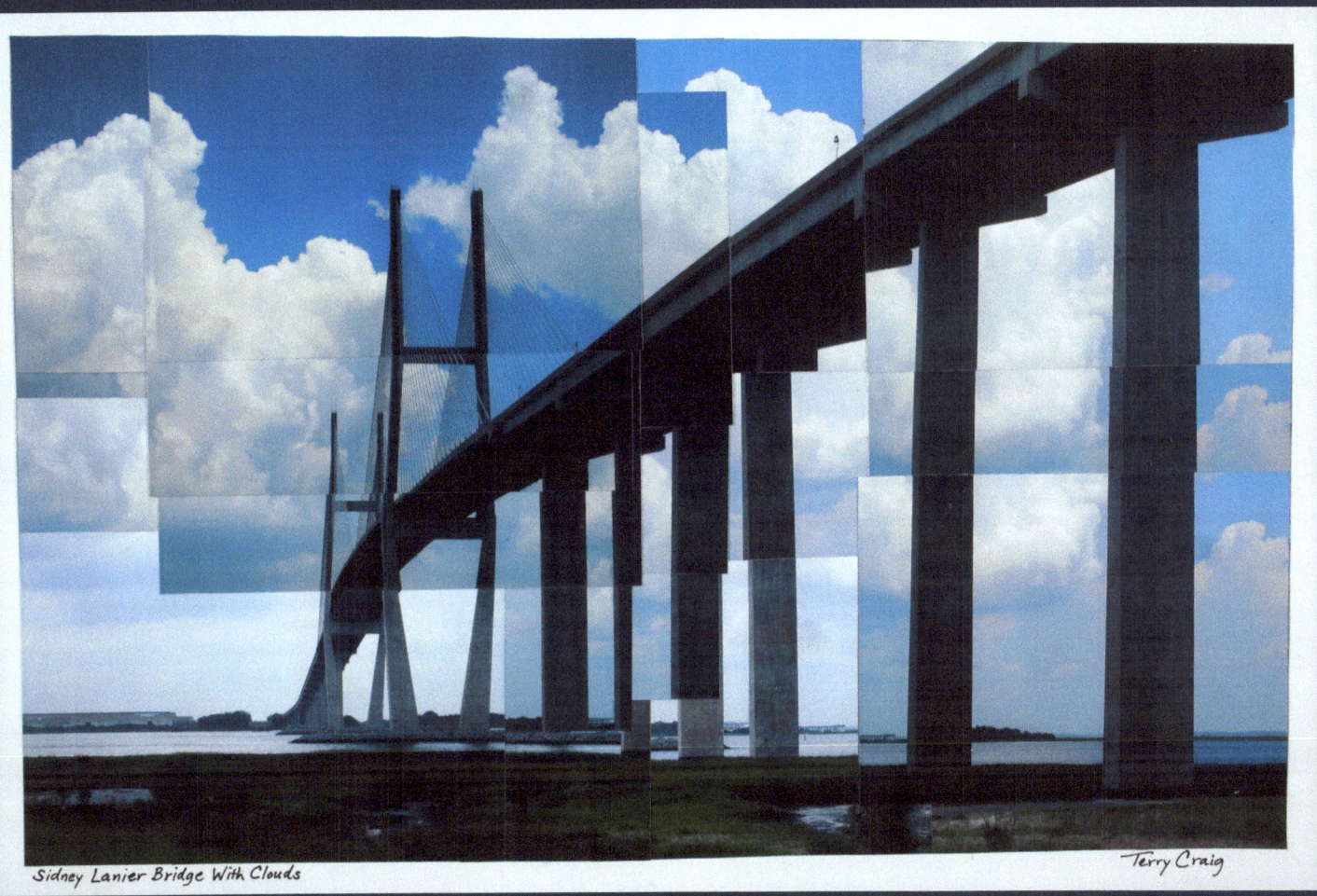

2010 | 12" x 18" | Photo collage on panel | $125.00

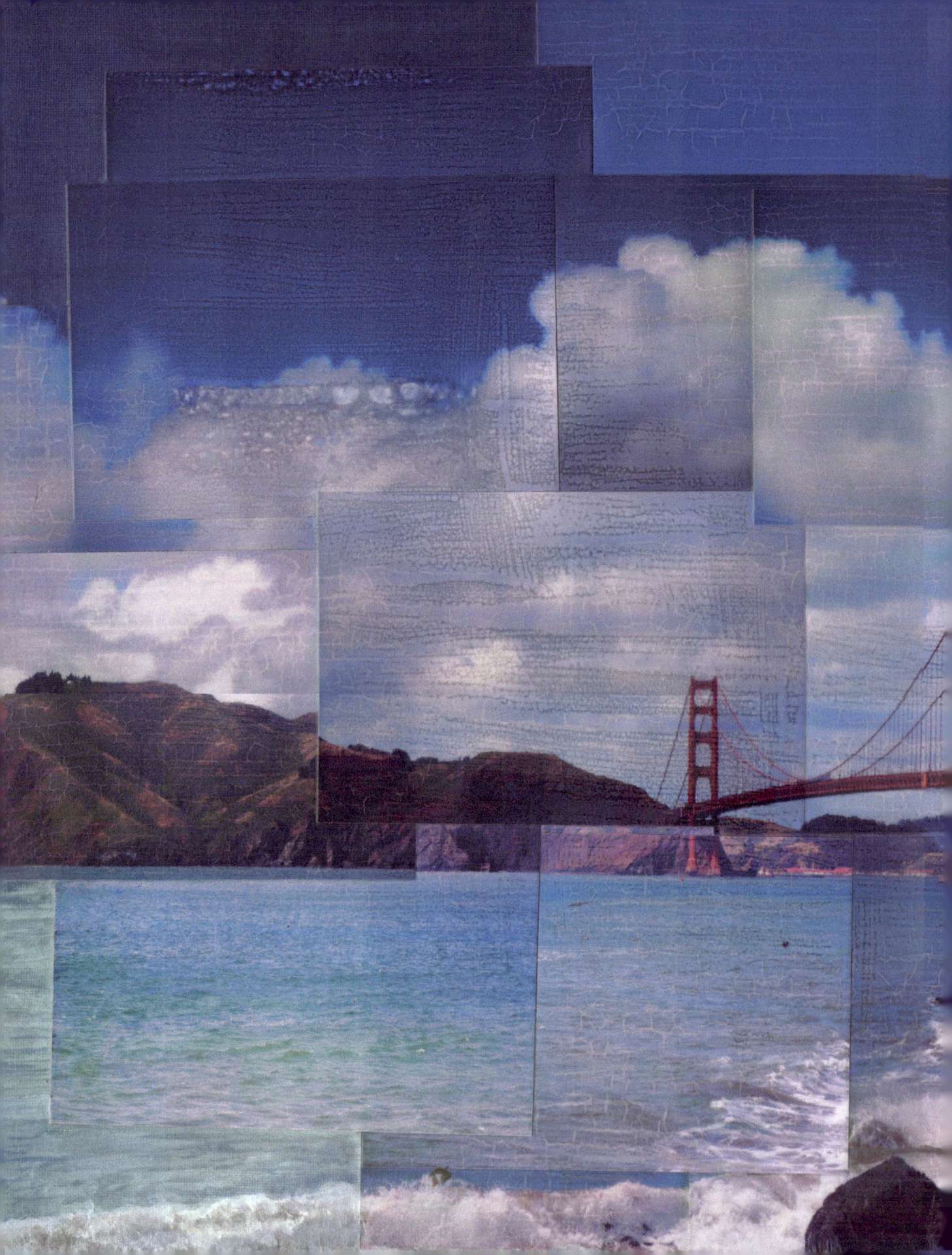

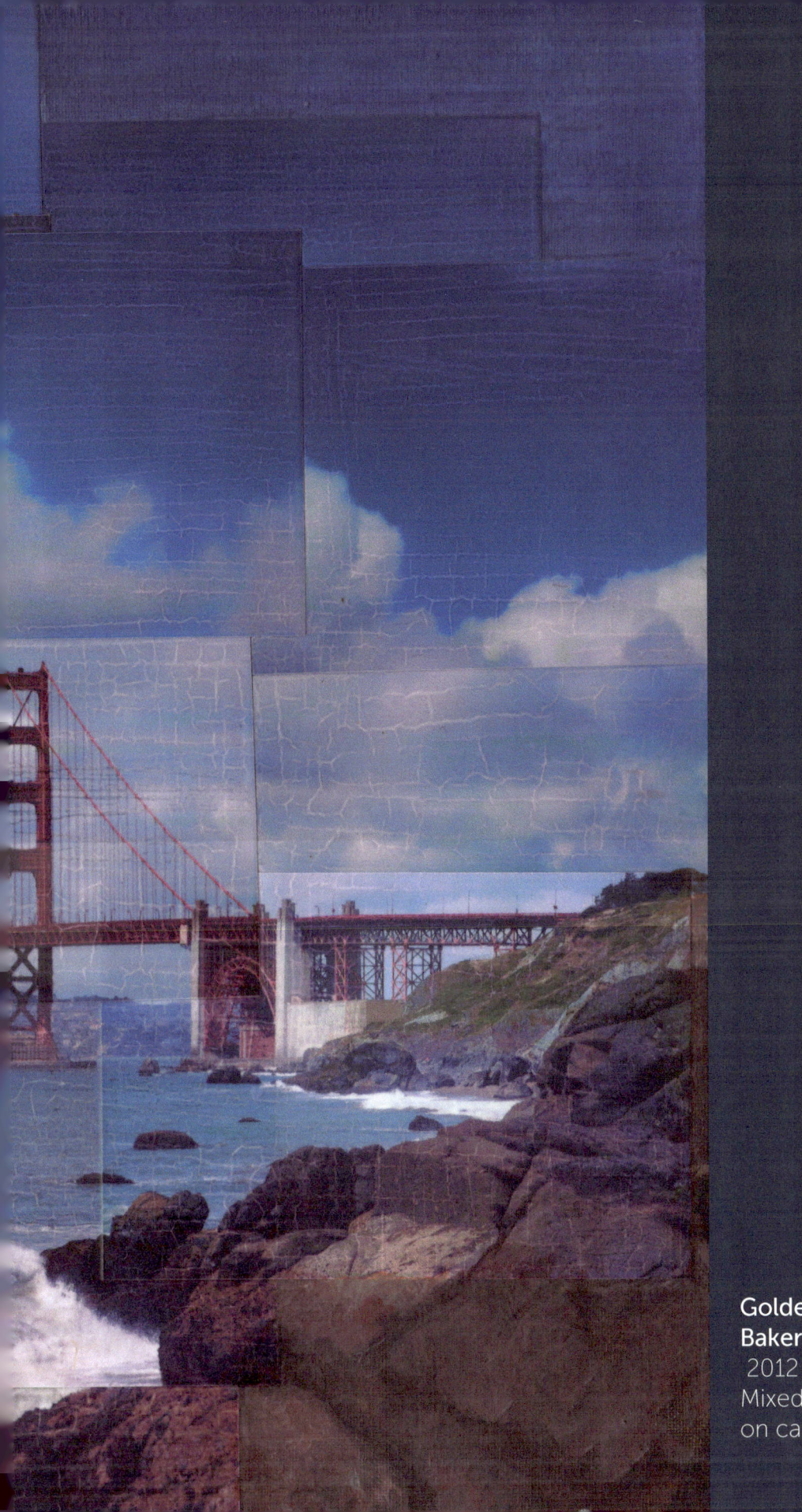

**Golden Gate Bridge from Baker Beach**
2012 | 16" x 20"
Mixed media photo collage on canvas | Sold

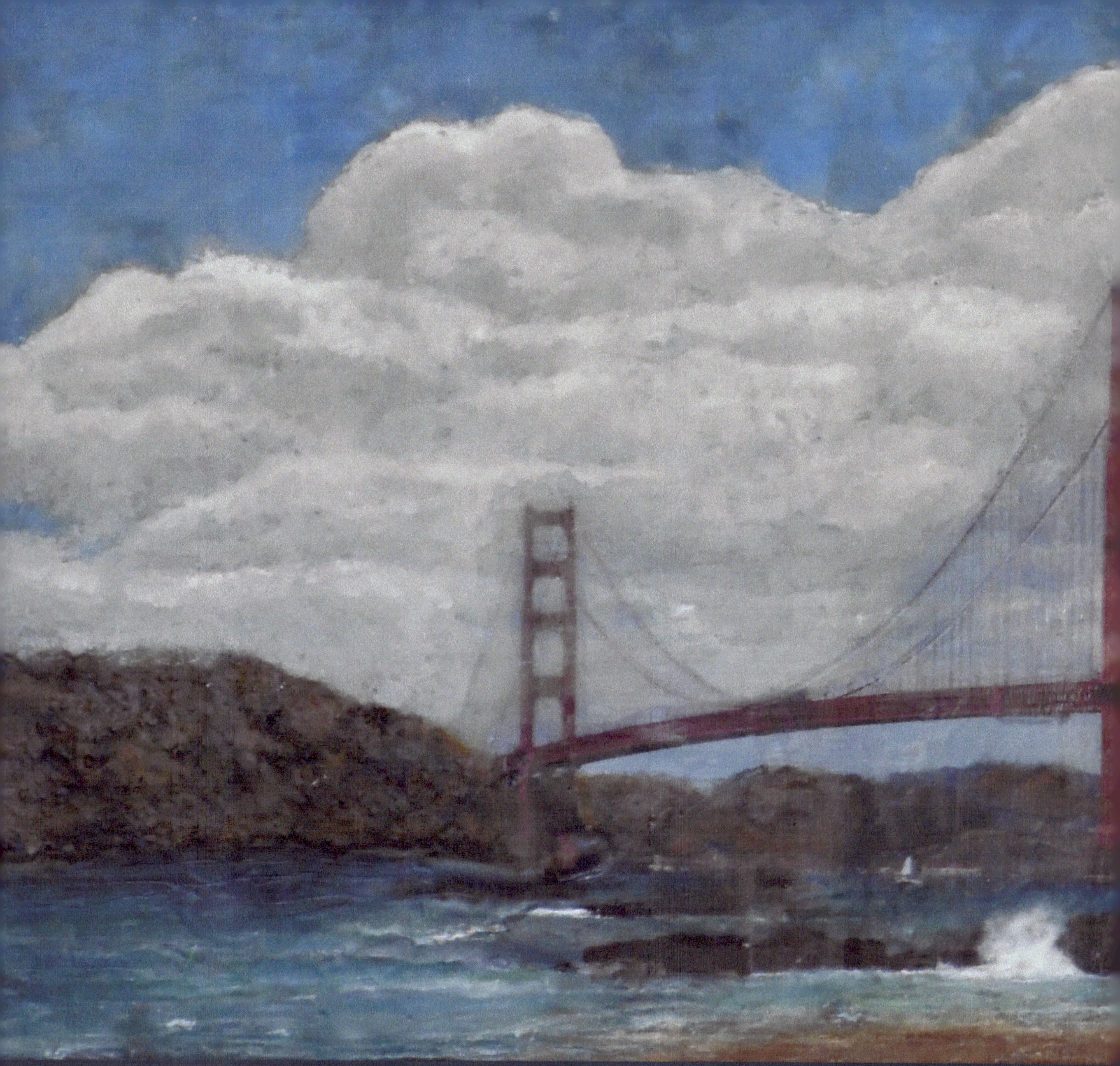

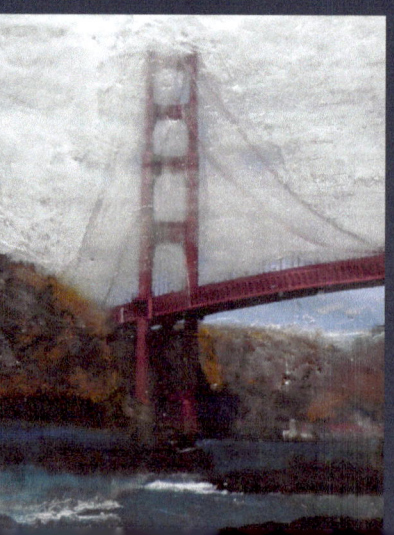

details

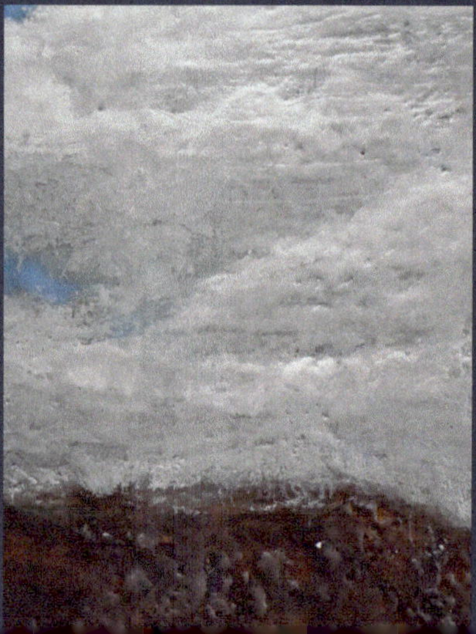

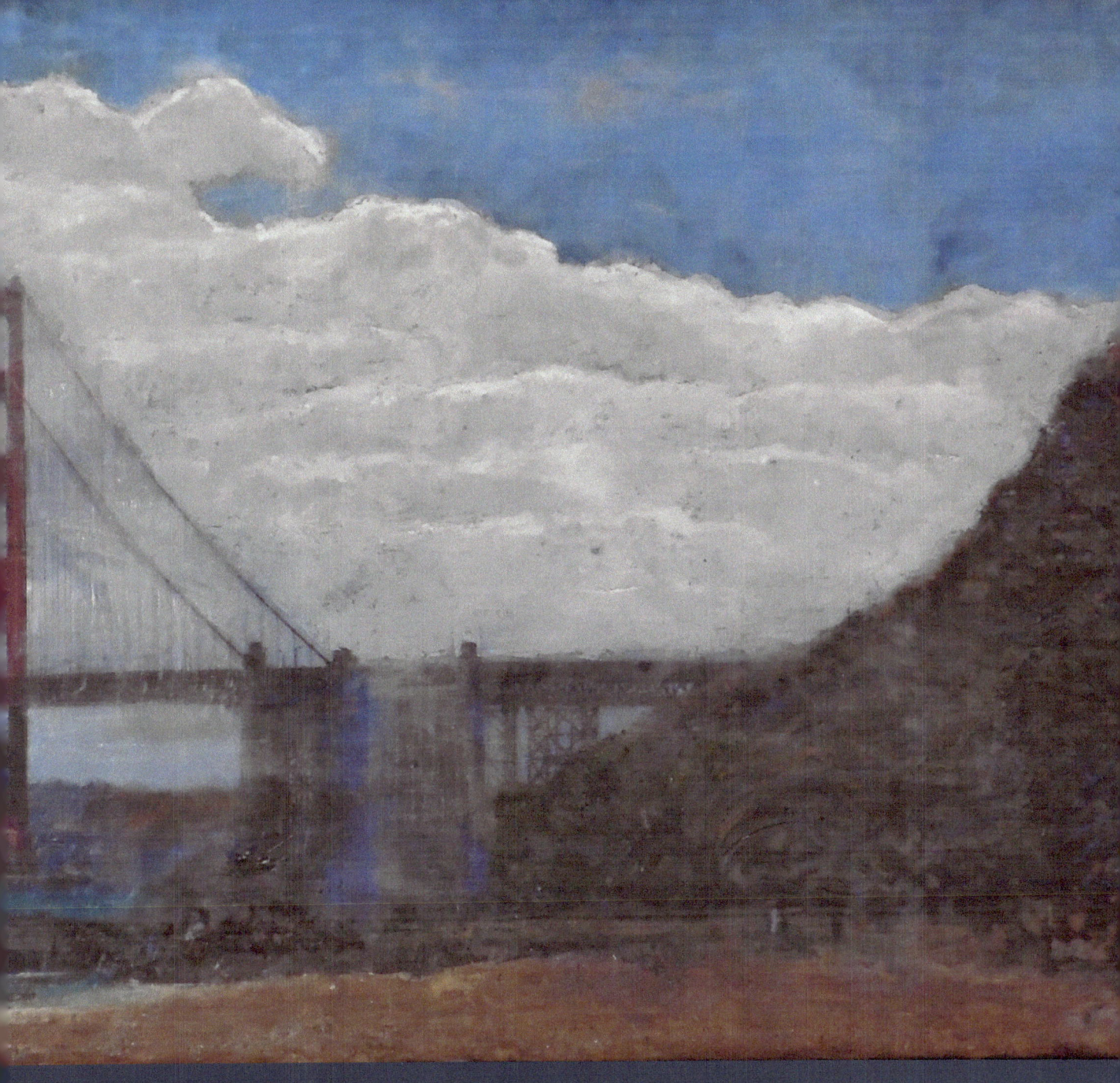

Baker Beach Golden Gate Panorama | 2017" | Photo encaustic on panel | 16" x 36" | $500.00

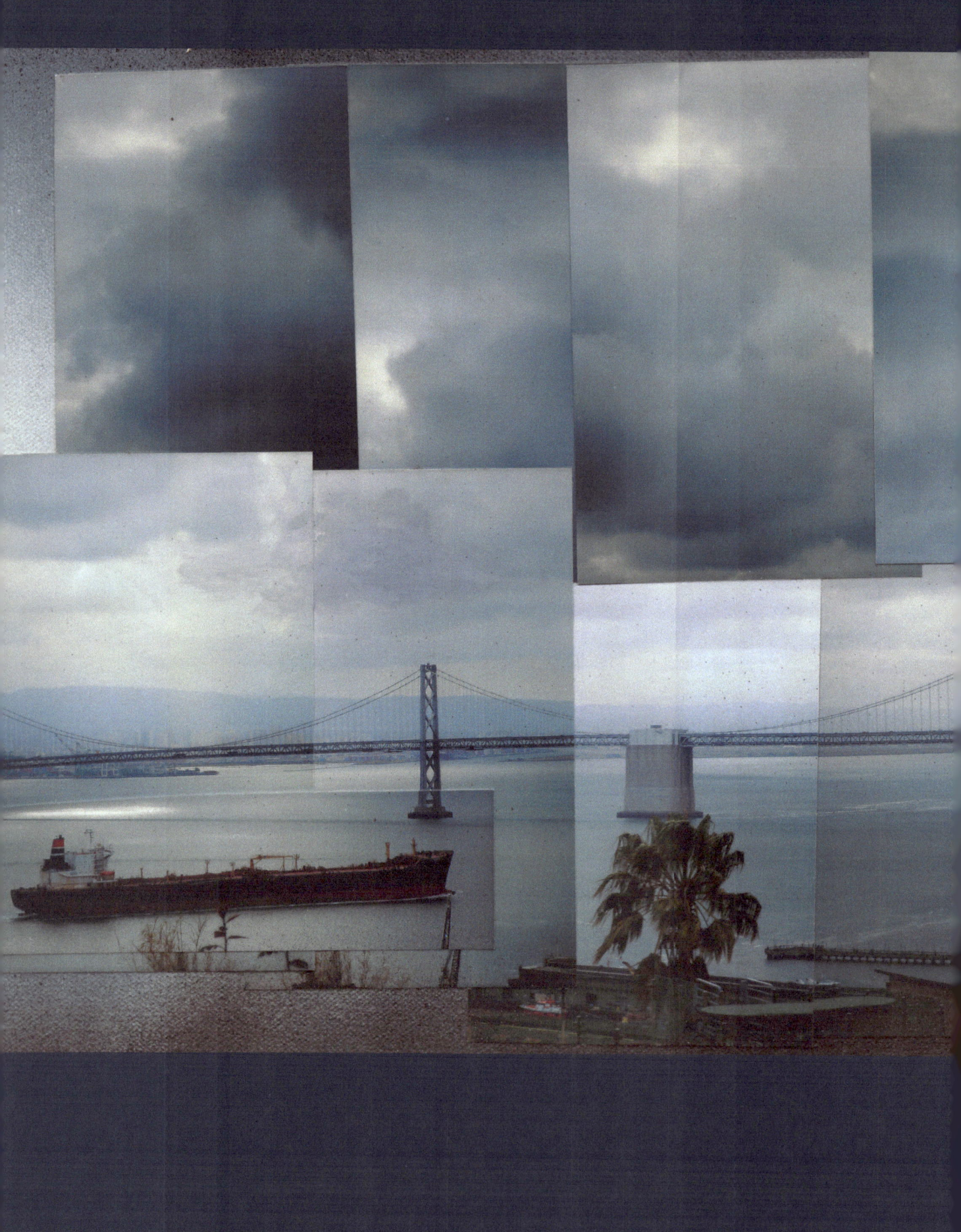

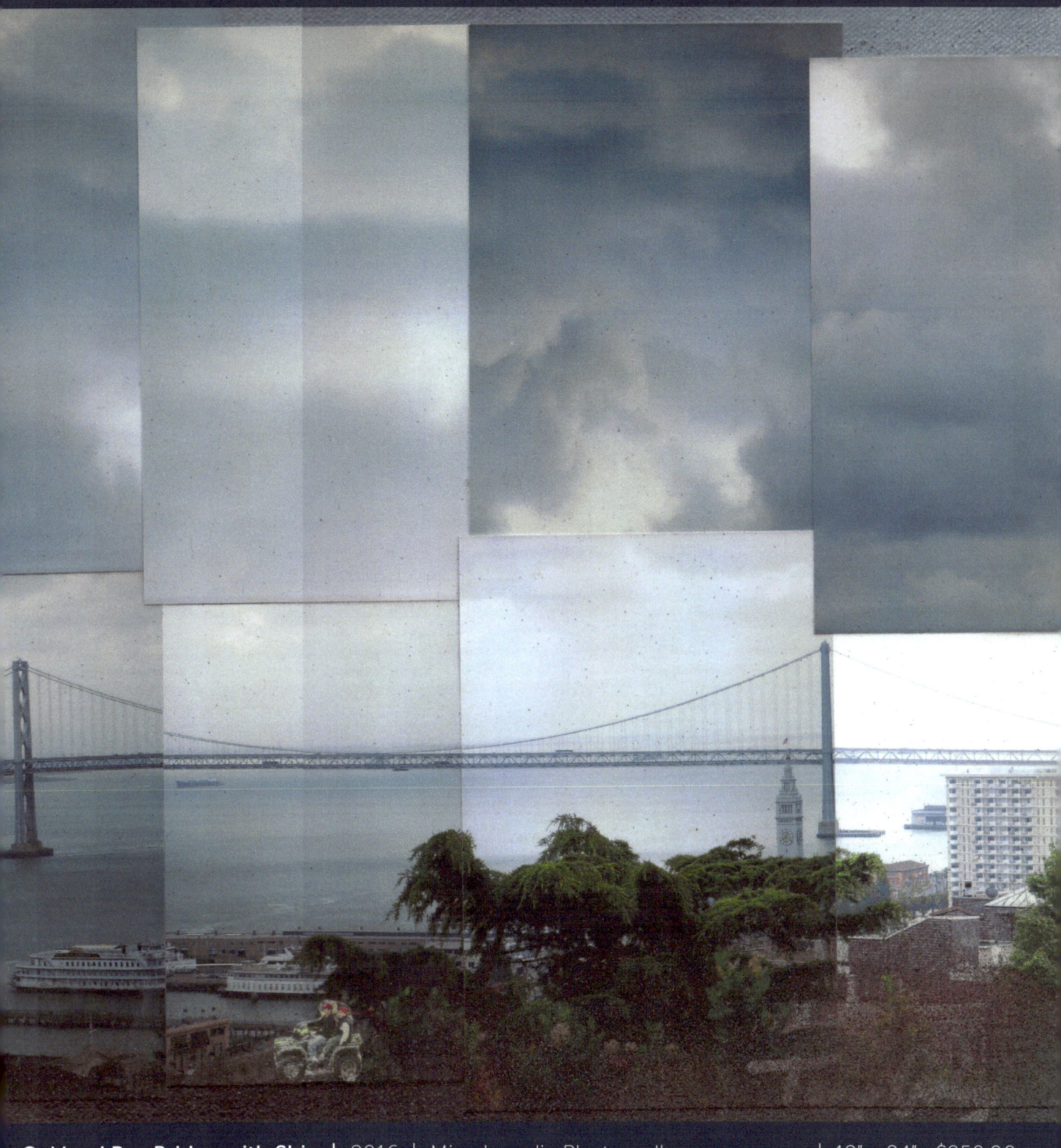

Oakland Bay Bridge with Ship | 2016 | Mixed media Photo collage on canvas | 12" x 24"  $250.00

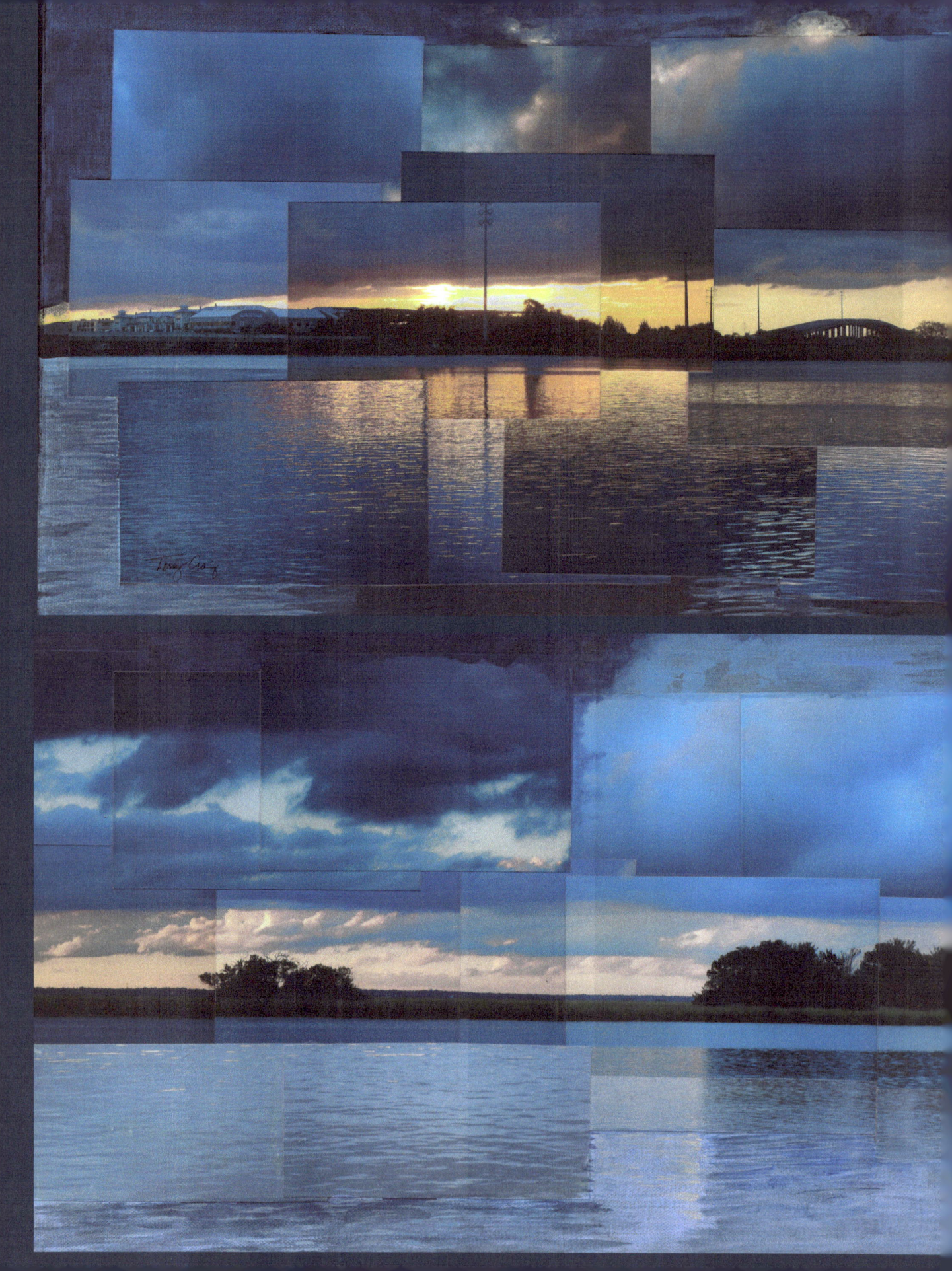

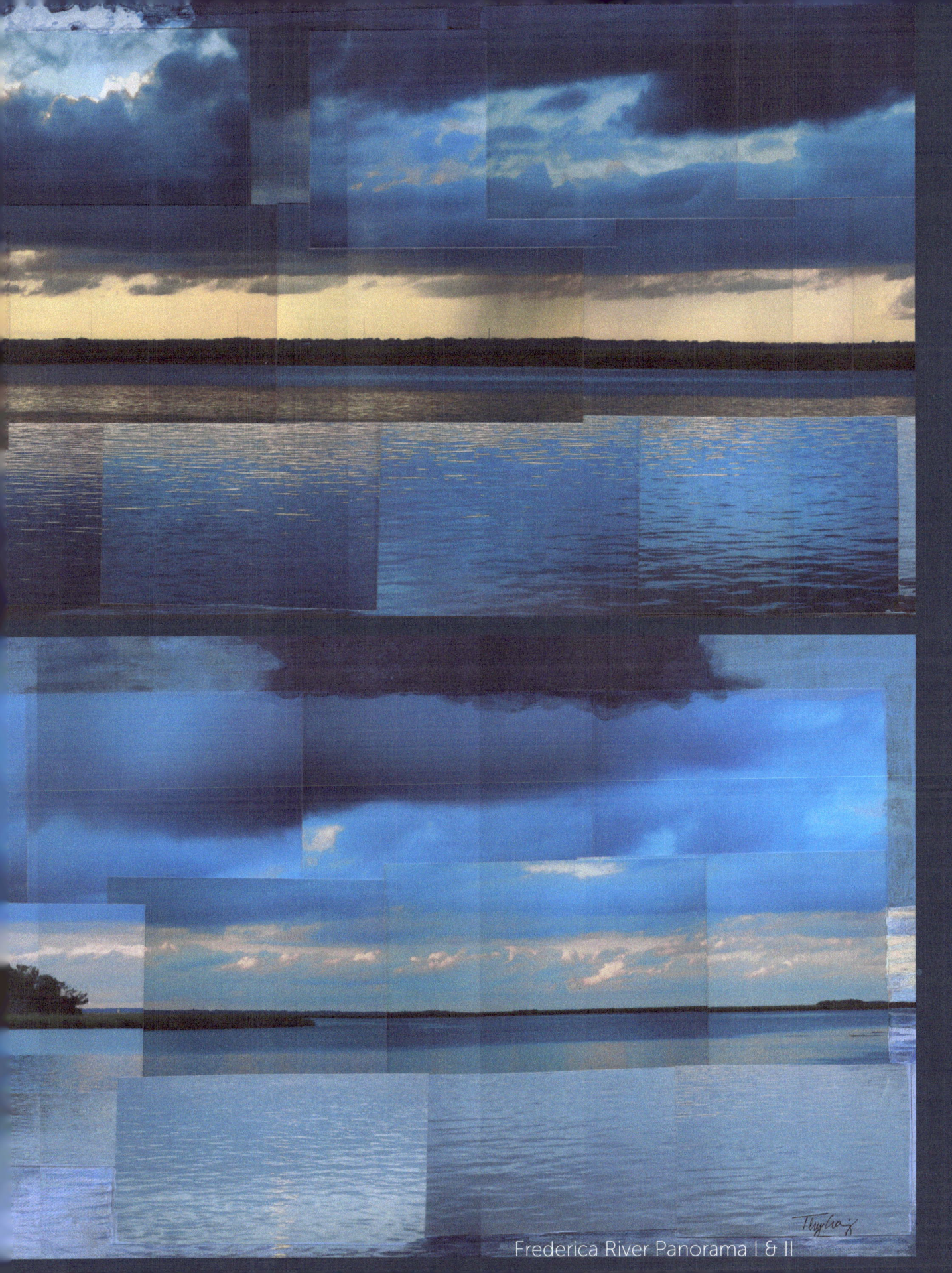
Frederica River Panorama I & II

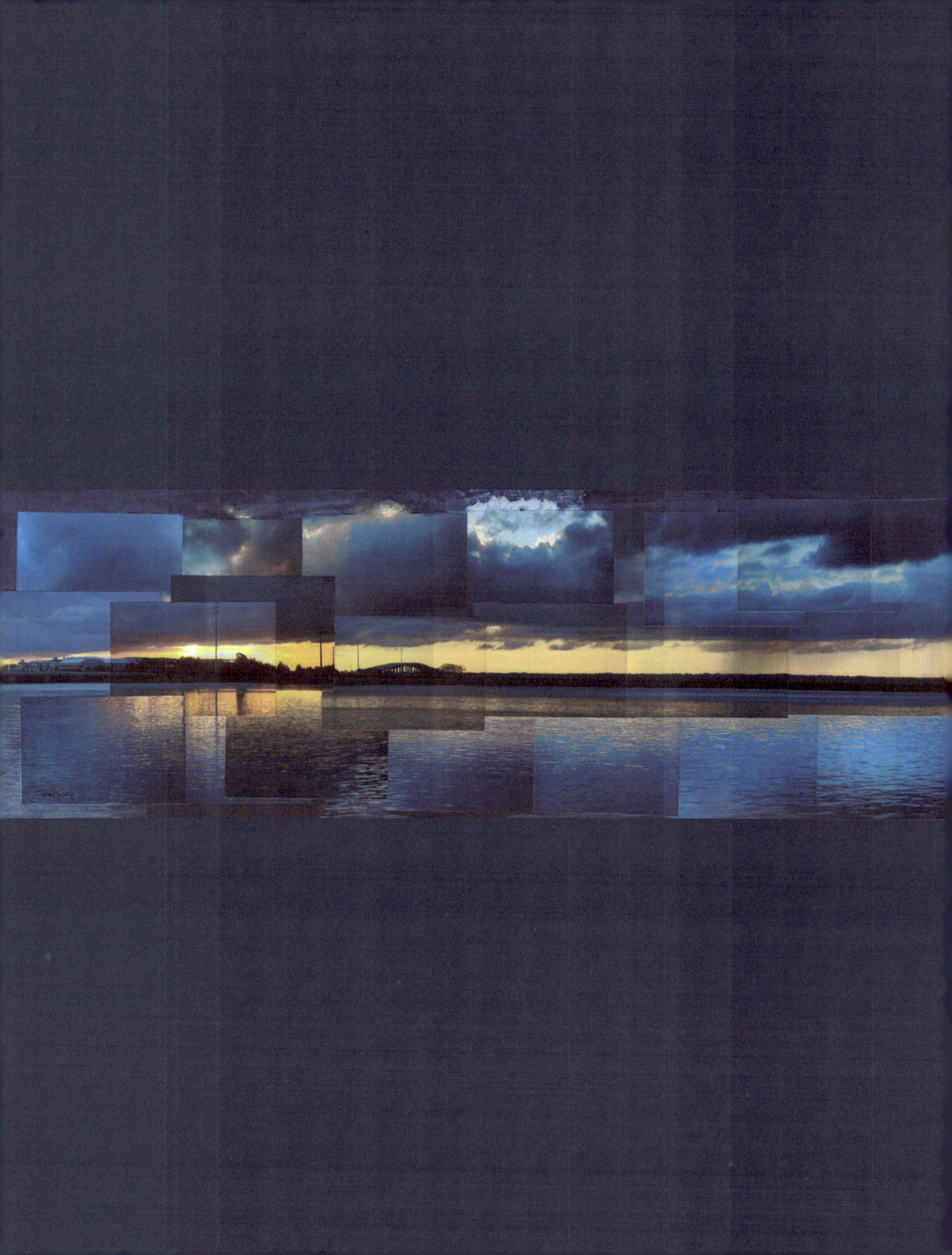

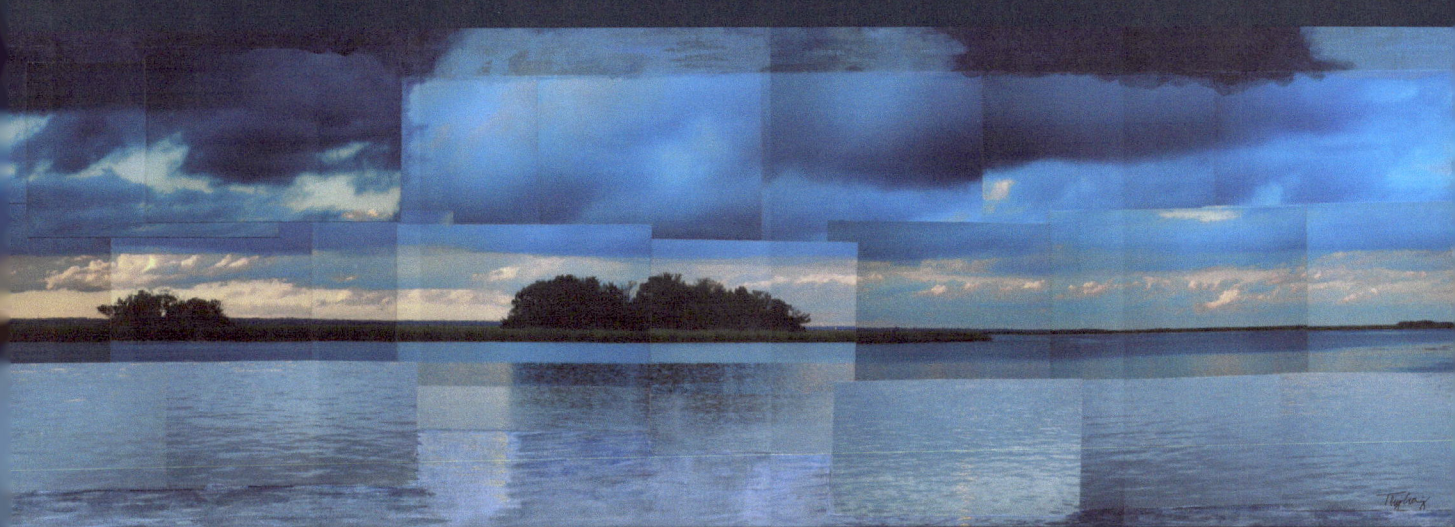

Frederica River Panorama I & II  |  12" X 72"  |  Mixed media Photo Collage  |  2013  |  Set - $600

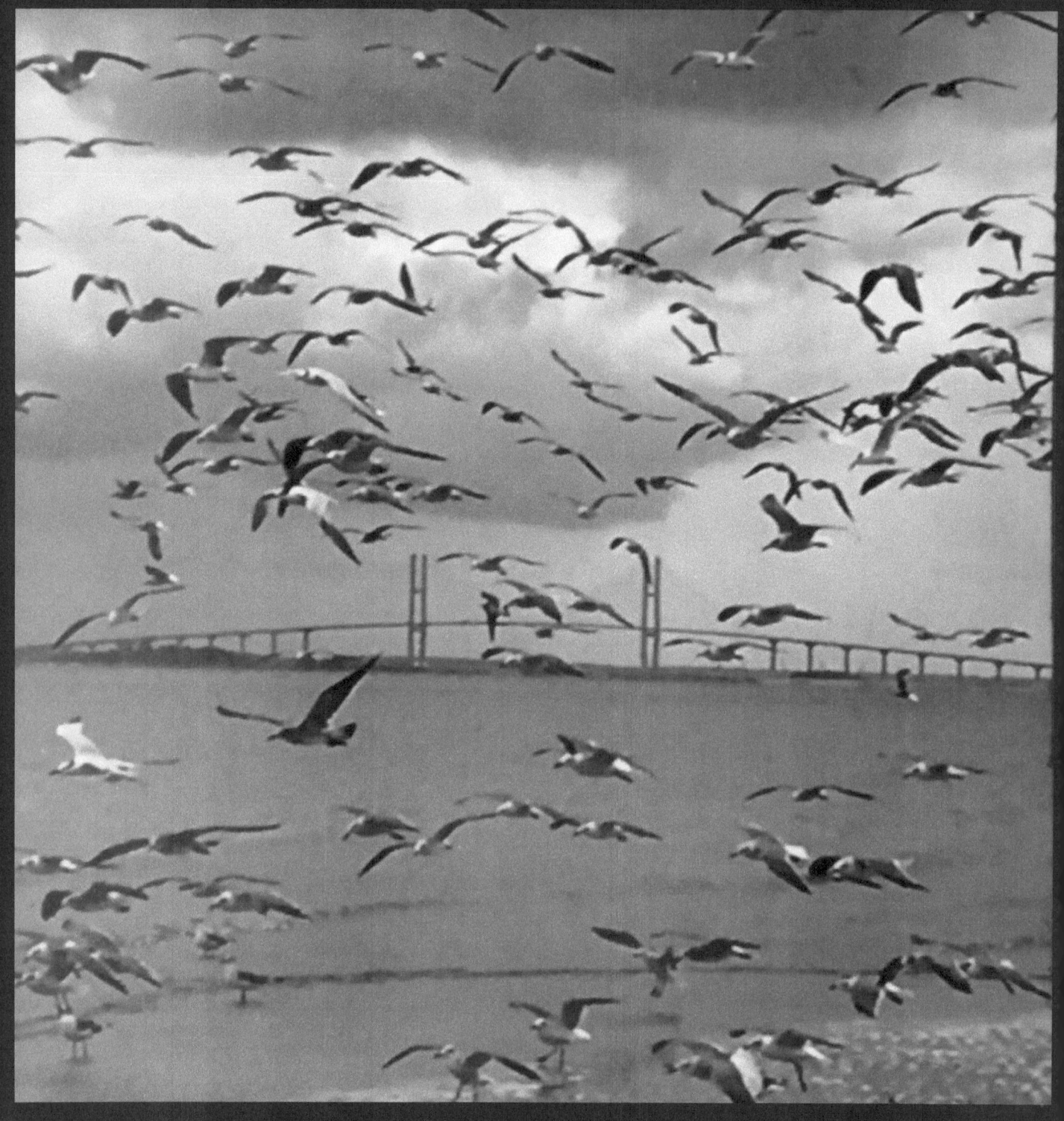

Sidney Lanier Bridge – Birds in Flight | 8"X8" | Photo on panel | 2017 | $80.00

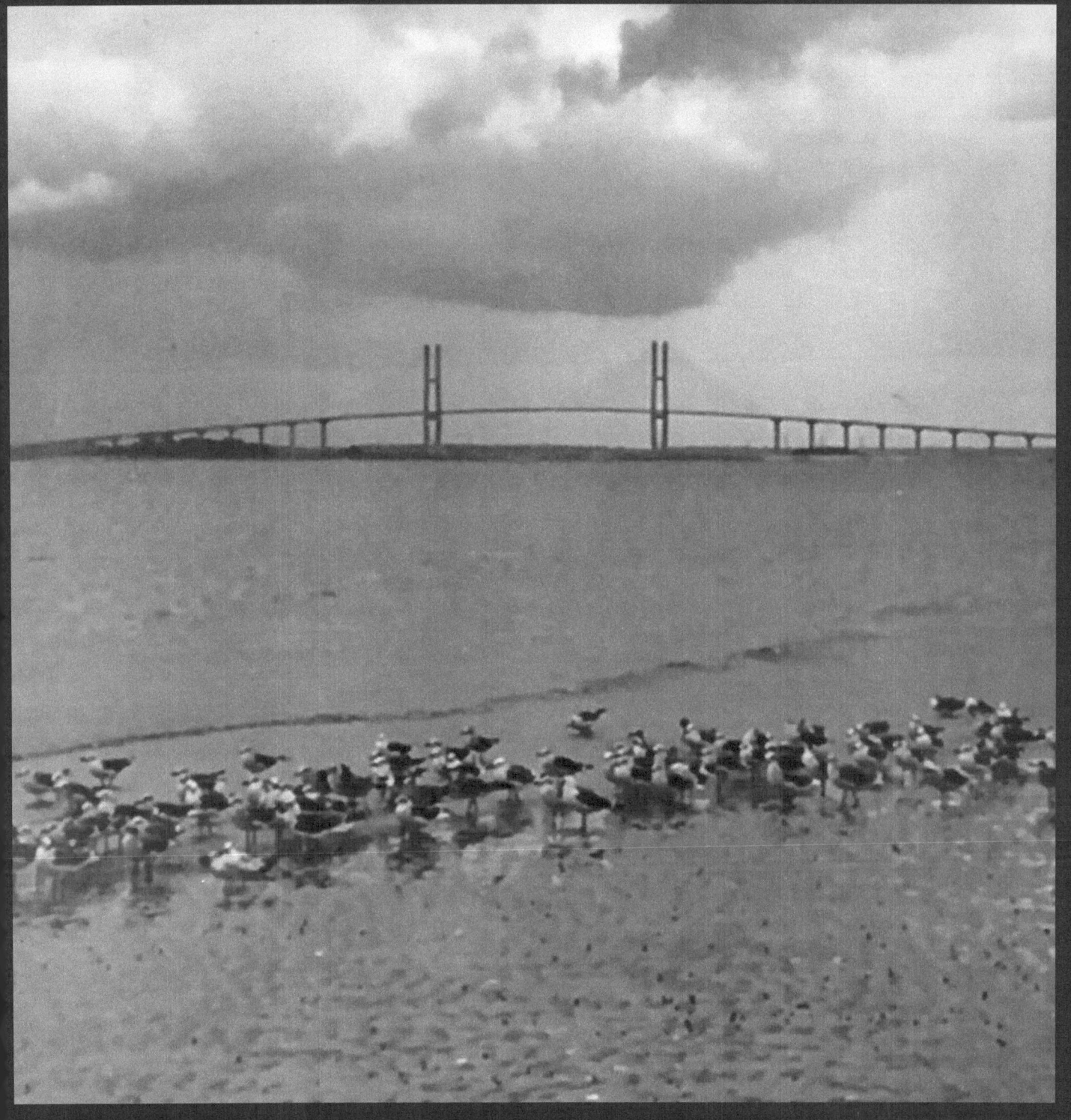

**Sidney Lanier Bridge – Birds at Rest** | 8"X 8" | Photo on panel | 2017 | $80.00

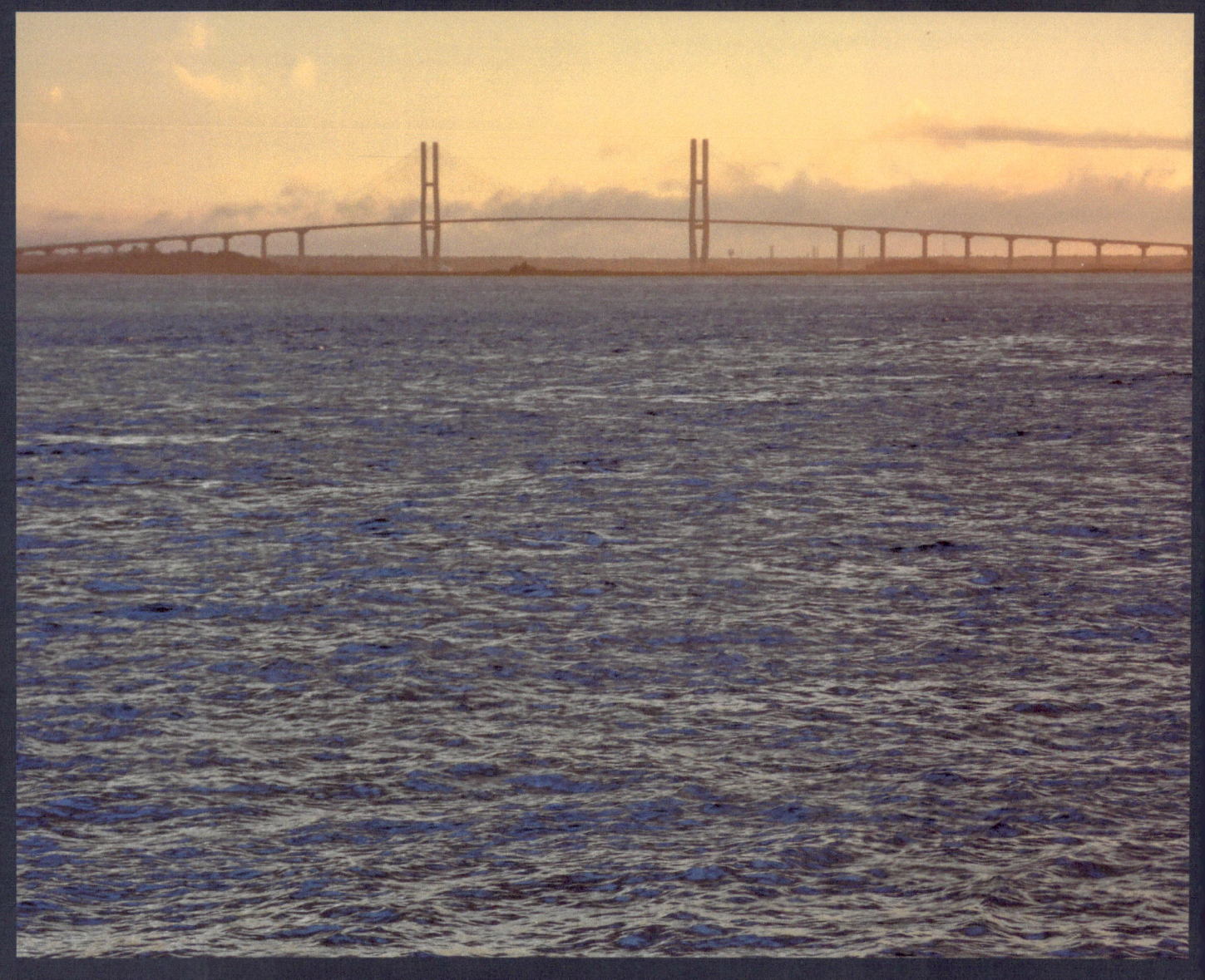

Sidney Lanier Bridge at Sunset | 6"X 6" | Photo on panel | 2017 | $65.00

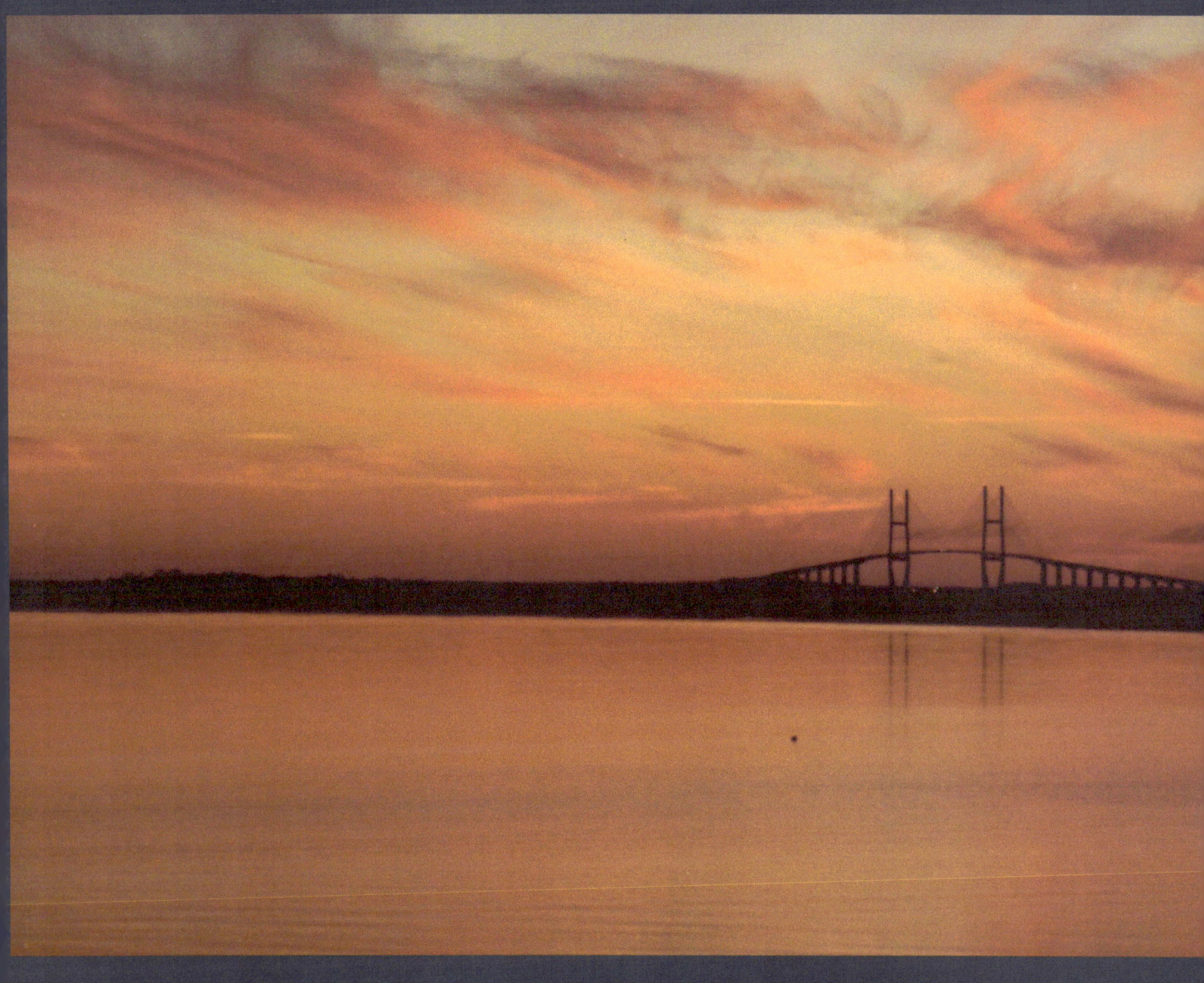

Sidney Lanier Bridge - Orange Sunset | 6"X 6" | Photo on panel | 2017 | $65.00

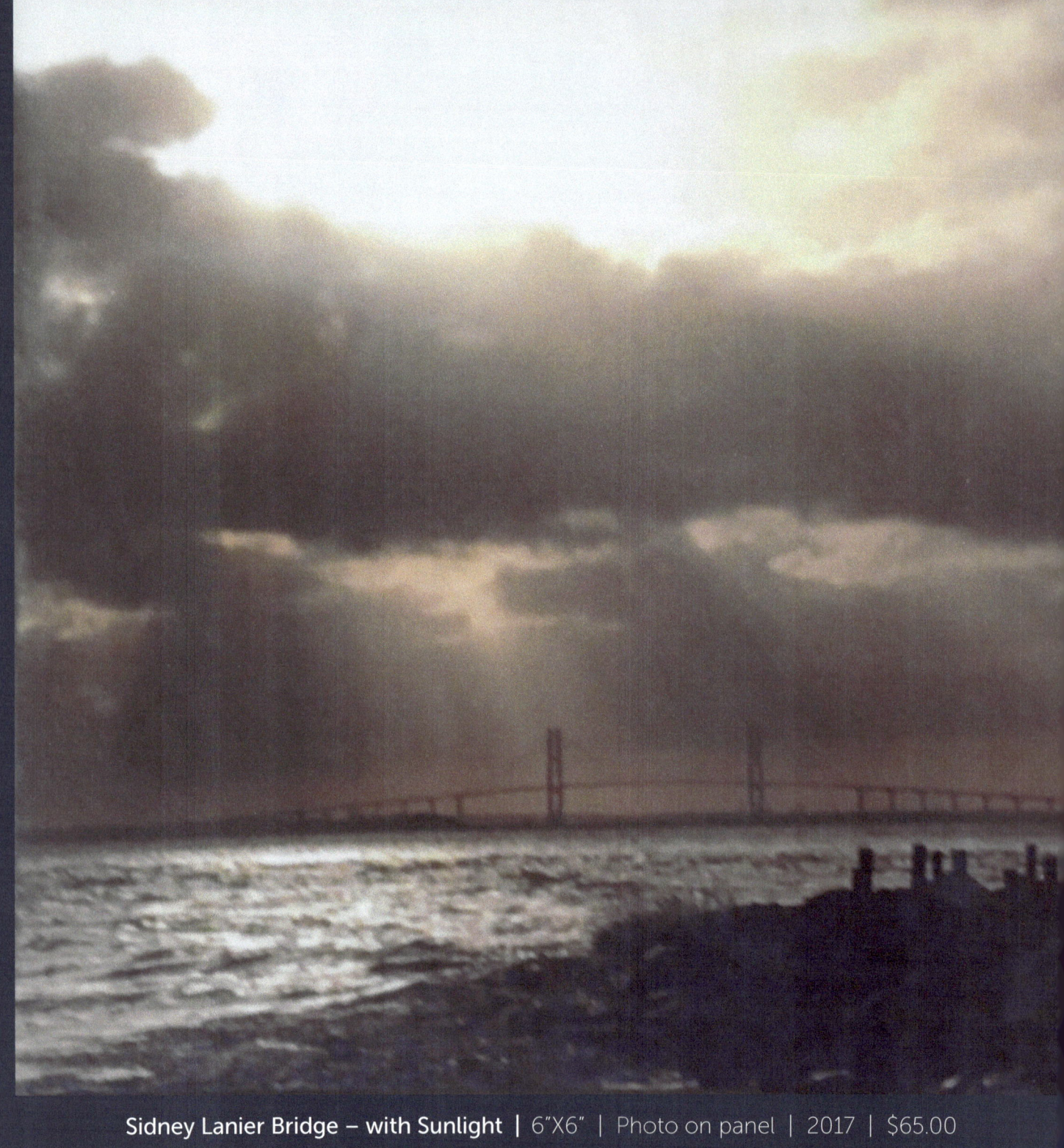

Sidney Lanier Bridge – with Sunlight | 6"X6" | Photo on panel | 2017 | $65.00

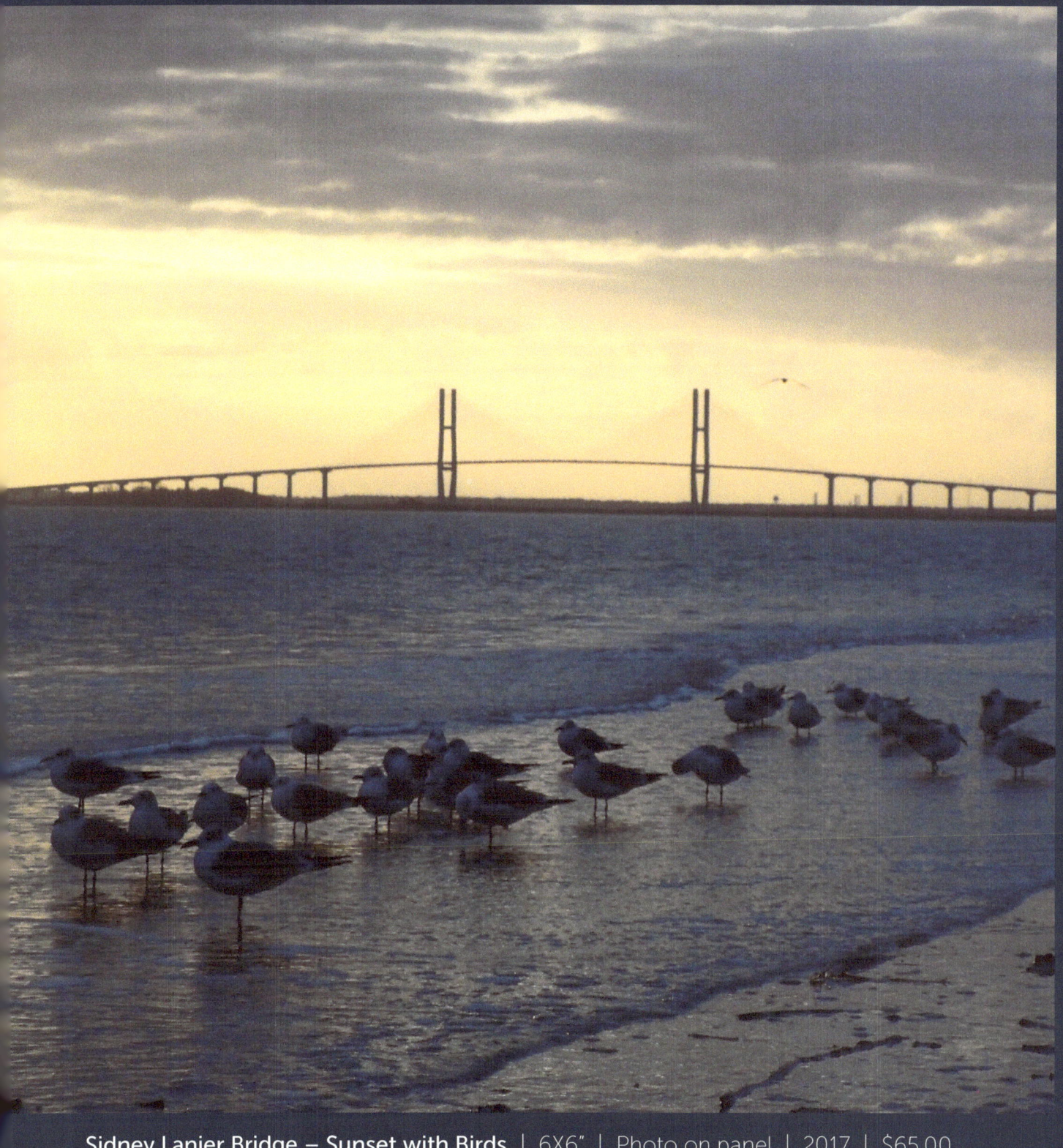

Sidney Lanier Bridge – Sunset with Birds | 6X6" | Photo on panel | 2017 | $65.00

ENCAUSTIC INFORMATION
by Terry Craig

The practice of painting with melted, pigmented beeswax is an ancient method that has experienced a revival in the contemporary world.

The Ancient World  -  The earliest known use of beeswax was by Greek shipbuilders who used it to
caulk the joints and hulls of their vesssels. Greek artists not only began to paint flat easel paintings, but
also for polychroming of clay and marble sculpture.

The Fayoum Portraits  -  The Greco-Roman communities of Egypt adopted a mixture of cultural practices that drew from the traditions of diverse backgrounds. A realistic life-size portrait was painted with colored wax and heated to fuse the picture on to a wooden panel (encaustic). The panel was kept as a portrait and became part of a mummy casing holding an embalmed body of the dead person. Some were painted during a person's lifetime and others were painted upon death. The dark, dry, airless tombs created a perfect environment for the encaustic paintings and most were perserved for 2,000 years in almost perfect condition.

Contemporary Encaustics  -  A few painters, such as  Diego Rivera, Arthur Dove and Karl Zerbe used encaustic, but it was the well-known Modernist painter Jasper Johns who brought the medium back to prominence. Johns wanted an expressive medium that didn't take long to dry. Johns began using encaustic in 1954 and had a monumental show of his encaustic work in 1958 at the Leo Castelli Gallery in New York City. Others began to use the medium to express their work. Brice Marden, Lynda Benglis, and Rachel Friedberg explored  the medium in different ways.  The sculptor, Nancy Graves and mixed-media artist Michelle Stuart added wax to their work. Since then, encaustic has exploded in use by many artists and photographers.

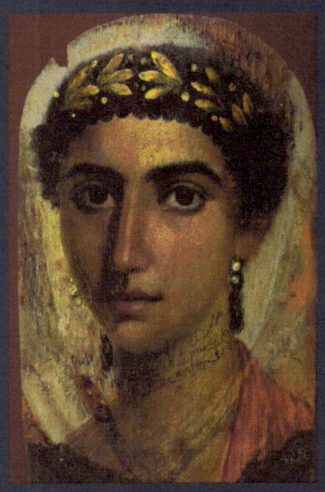

Roman Fayoum Portrait
100 B.C. - 200 A.D.

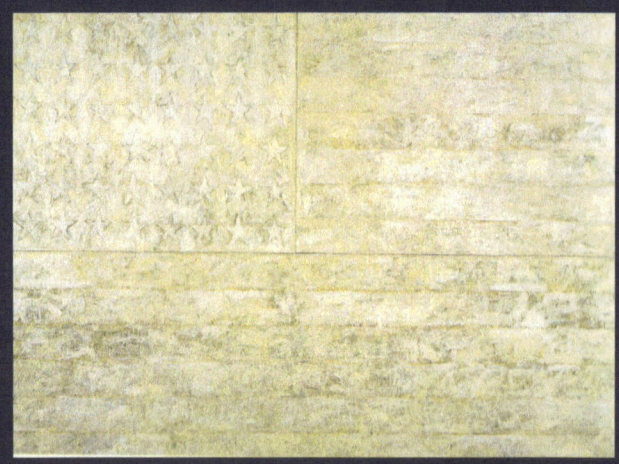

White Flag. Jasper Johns. 1955.

I began to use wax with my photographs for texture and an added sense of mystery and interest. Wax makes my photographs translucent and allows me to work with the surface to add layers of marks and meaning. To see more of my photocollage and photoencaustic work, go to our family art website, www.craigarthouse.com.

(Text excerpted from The Art of Encaustic Painting. Joanne Mattera. 2001. Watson-Guptil NY)

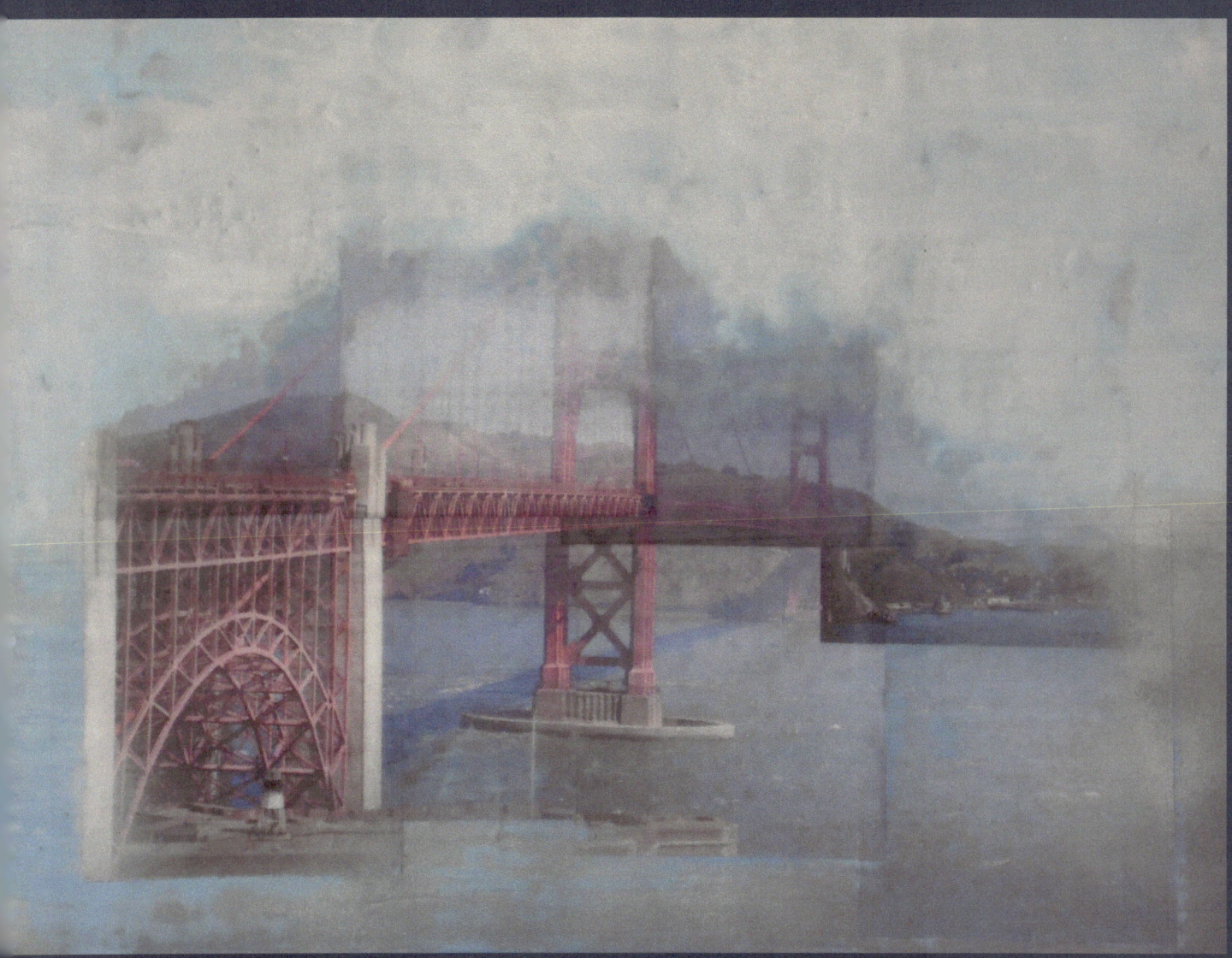

**Golden Gate Bridge in the Fog**  |  2017  |  Photo encaustic on panel  |  12" x 16"  |  $200.00

www.ingramcontent.com/pod-product-compliance
Lightning Source LLC
Chambersburg PA
CBHW040408220526
45473CB00004B/1172